"An important step-change in how we think about research inclusion and democratisation in counselling and psychotherapy".

Angela Sweeney, *Senior Lecturer in User-Led Research, King's College London*

"Much has been written about ethics in counselling and psychotherapy, but it is rare to encounter a book written with such a depth of practice experience and academic insight whilst honouring what ethics truly means in the context of participatory research: Nothing about us without us! The message is clear: participatory research is driven by an intention to overcome injustice and support respectful, inclusive, and relational ways through which people who may have quite different backgrounds, goals, values and skills can live together. Presented here is a text that has short, focused chapters supported by vivid examples, learning activities, and which contains welcome references as well as suggestions for further reading. This is truly an indispensable straightforward introductory guide for anyone seeking to develop a better appreciation of the strengths, limitations and application of participatory research in counselling, psychotherapy and allied professions".

Divine Charura, *Professor of Counselling Psychology, School of Education, Language and Psychology, York St John University*

"This latest book by John and Julia McLeod delves into the intricacies of collaborative participatory research that aims to reconfigure the stances of power and privilege that shape how knowledge is generated and interpreted. *Ethics in Participatory Research on Counselling and Psychotherapy* not only offers an incredible depth of scholarship and information, it is also inspiring and encourages the enrichment of research approaches by giving voice to marginalized and overlooked perspectives. The ethical and engaged consideration leads the reader to reflect on their own relationship with research and knowledge generation. I predict that the book will become a *go to* reference point for anybody conducting research in counselling and psychotherapy".

Ladislav Timulak, *Counselling psychologist and practicing therapist; involved in the training of future practitioners and researchers as Professor in Counselling Psychology at Trinity College Dublin, Ireland.*

"An amazing and thought-provoking exploration of the concepts and methods of participatory research. The authors advocate a simple, yet often unfulfilled idea: all research should aim to be clinically meaningful, ethically responsible, and do justice to participants' perspectives. Instead of being yet another textbook on research methods, this book opens new avenues for researcher reflection, creativity, and humility in relation to the challenges presented by an ever-evolving human world".

Tomáš Řiháček, Ph.D., *Professor of Psychology and Head of Centre for Psychotherapy Research at Masaryk University, Brno, Czech Republic.*

"This important and enlightening book takes us a step further from the days when research participants were 'subjects' to their involvement as active, engaged, and empowered collaborators. Participatory enquiry is at the leading edge of developments in the counselling and psychotherapy research field, and McLeod and McLeod give a practical, informative, and comprehensive guide to establishing the ethical foundations for this work".

Mick Cooper, *Professor of Counselling Psychology, Roehampton University, London*

"Participatory research methods are the ones that my students are most excited to learn. McLeod and McLeod present these methods with a passion that is inspiring and also with an honesty and openness that makes participatory research approachable. As leading scholars in psychotherapy and counselling research, they attend to fine points of method that further the methodological integrity of projects as well as their potential to further social justice ends".

Heidi M. Levitt, *Professor, Department of Psychology, University of Massachusetts Boston, Editor, Qualitative Psychology and author of Essentials of Critical-Constructivist Grounded Theory and Reporting Qualitative Research in Psychology.*

"Psychotherapy research offers limited benefit to clients and therapists unless it is grounded in their perspectives; that is, unless it is truly participatory. So far, such research is in short supply. Enter John and Julia McLeod, who offer their readers an introduction to participatory research grounded in a compelling ethical framework. The authors write vividly, using jargon-free language and evocative examples. How rare to find a book on research that is a pleasure to read. Readers will come away inspired and equipped to participate in research that matters".

Lisa A. Goodman, *Clinical-community psychologist and Professor and Training Director in the Department of Counseling and Applied Developmental Psychology at Boston College. She uses a community-based participatory research approach to explore intimate partner violence, social justice pedagogy, and healing practices that extend beyond the 50-minute hour in counselling psychology.*

"John and Julia McLeod shed scholarly light on areas long neglected in psychotherapy and counselling research, and discuss why it took so long for these practices to flow toward the mainstream. This book not only provides great insight and practical detail on the rationales for participatory research approaches across a range of specific therapy topics. It also, with the extraordinary strength of a friendly-toned, well-read, and clinically experienced perspective, situates therapy and therapy research as practice communities within their relevant social and moral contexts. I recommend this book as a brilliant resource for both young and experienced researchers".

Christian Moltu, *Head of Research, Division of Psychiatry, Førde Hospital Trust. Professor of Clinical Psychology, Western Norway University of Applied Science*

"I wish this book had been available before I did my participatory research with NHS psychotherapy clients on Complex PTSD because it would have saved me a lot of time and trouble! It will be an invaluable resource for any therapist or trainee who believes that clients need to have a voice in research in order to make that research credible—central priority in relation to the democratisation of the research enterprise".

Dr Catherine Matheson, *EMDR Consultant, Supervisor in Psychodynamic Psychotherapy, practising in south London*

"This book is a trailblazer, filled with compelling insights and practical advice. The authors masterfully introduce participatory research through a blend of storytelling and actionable steps. It's a beacon of ethical wisdom and an invaluable resource. Part of the *Ethics in Action* series, it bridges gaps between disciplines, promoting social justice and inclusivity. It's engaging and transformative, fostering collaboration within research and enhancing ethical awareness through a pluralistic lens—a must-read!"

Dr Marcella Finnerty,
IICP College President, Dublin

"This book brings a much-needed paradigm shift—setting a next stage after the evidence-based approach to psychotherapy research and practice. Participatory research broadens the focus of research in counselling and psychotherapy by including perspectives of service users, clients, carer, and members of society who are directly and indirectly affected by it. It provides a wholistic view of research by aligning scientific rigor with a variety of social justice goals. The book is highly valuable for researchers, instructors, and both graduate and undergraduate students in all areas of helping professions and will contribute to developing future research that is scientifically rigorous and socially transformative".

Shigeru Iwakabe, *Professor of Clinical Psychology, Ritsumeikan University, Japan; President of the International Society for Psychotherapy Research*

"I am confident that *Ethics in Participatory Research on Counselling and Psychotherapy: Justice, Solidarity and Care* will prove a cherished resource, for students of research right through to seasoned academics. John and Julia McLeod connect with their audience through a direct and common-sense writing style, informed by a deep engagement with the experience of those whose project and program examples bring the book's ideas to life. The pluralistic ethic advanced here is distinctive and offers a frame through which to capture the complexity of the moral landscapes researchers find themselves operating within".

John Hills, *Head of Programme for MSc/Dip Integrative Psychotherapy, Metanoia Institute, London*

"An excellent resource for students, novice and experienced practitioners, researchers and policy makers. How can we involve non-professional people in the process of designing and conducting research? John and Julia McLeod's book provides a series of chapters exploring various aspects of participatory research offering many examples and further reading in this field. Every chapter ends with questions for reflection and discussion (to consolidate ones reading, explore ideas in a reading group, discuss in classrooms). Some concepts that are elaborated and I have found profoundly important (and at times moving) are: resistance to systems of government and colonialist and capitalist exploitation, indigenous and affirming values, a more than human world that sustained all life, moral injury, counterstorytelling, power, privilege and inequality in academic research, democratization of the critical dialogical process inherent in the values of scientific research, ways of knowing in kinship with land and people, decolonizing research and practice, the problem with averages (much of existing privileged research) is that it conceals uniqueness and further 'minoritizes' and silences groups, overreliance on one's perspective leads to silencing of voices with valuable insights. Participatory research has at its heart caring, kindness, honest and transparency. Learnings from this book can be incorporated into routine therapy practice offering new ways of working with clients damaged by social injustices. When participatory research qualities and concepts are embedded in practice, clients and groups can benefit hugely by being heard empowered and privileged in reconstructing and reclaiming their life stories. Participatory research has a pluralistic ethical stance where decision-making is negotiated considering values and traditions of communities. The book is beautifully written immediate and accessible to all readers. I wholeheartedly endorse this book and hope many people have the opportunity to read it".

Sophia Balamoutsou, *Coach, Counsellor, Supervisor, Researcher, Trainer: Institute of Agri-Food and Life Sciences, Hellenic Mediterranean University Research Centre, Heraklion, Crete, Greece.*

"*Ethics in Participatory Research on Counselling and Psychotherapy* by John and Julia McLeod provides an informative and impressive overview of participatory research in relation to its findings, its methods, and the inevitable ethical challenges associated with it. They bring an ethics of solidarity and care into the research context together with the necessity of respect and equality at every step of the research process. Running through the book is sensitivity towards and practical concern with issues of power, and the abolition of colonialisation and marginalisation within research. The scope of this book goes beyond participatory research and speaks to decisive and necessary aspects of any research process: it should be on the desk of every researcher".

Rolf Sundet, *Emeritus Professor, Centre for Mental Health and Substance Abuse, University of South-Eastern Norway*

"Written by two of the most significant voices in modern counselling and psychotherapy, this book provides a much-needed resource for understanding not only the importance of participatory research in contemporary society, but how to undertake it. Readers will enjoy the highly engaging and accessible walk through key considerations and features of their approach, learning how meaningful research can be carried out ethically, relationally, and responsively, and serve to enrich our knowledge through a variety of perspectives: therapeutic, social, and cultural. It is a ground-breaking book, and an essential one for anyone wishing to undertake inclusive research with a pluralistic lens".

Kate Smith, *Professor of Education., School of Education, University of Aberdeen*

Ethics in Participatory Research on Counselling and Psychotherapy: Justice, Solidarity and Care

Increasingly, therapy practitioners and researchers position themselves within a pluralistic perspective that draws on the value of multiple sources of knowledge. The aim of this book is to highlight the distinctive ethical challenges and opportunities associated with a pluralistic research orientation.

The book begins by succinctly summarising ethical concepts and strategies, such as informed consent, confidentiality, and avoidance of harm, that form the foundations of ethically sound research. An overview of distinctive ethical features of pluralistic research is then provided, followed by a series of chapters that address specific strands of ethics work. The closing chapter discusses approaches to training and ethical inquiry, the establishment of communities of research practice, and the provision of forms of counselling and psychotherapy that promote social justice. Each chapter will open with a concise chapter outline and close with a summary of key learning points, take-home skills, and follow-up learning activities. Case examples from published studies will be used to illustrate how theory and concepts have been implemented in real-life investigative contexts.

Written in plain English that is accessible to a wide range of readers, with recommended reading signposted in respect of advanced topics, this book will be an essential resource for practicing and trainee professionals and researchers in the psychological professions.

John McLeod is a counselling educator, researcher, and author who is committed to the development of flexible, co-created ways of working together in therapy that build on client strengths and resources. He has published widely on a range of topics associated with research in counselling and psychotherapy that allows clients to express their views on the therapy they have received.

Julia McLeod is an experienced practitioner, educator, and researcher in the field of counselling and psychotherapy, currently based at the University of Aberdeen. She has particular interests in embedded counselling, pluralistic approaches to therapy, and the use of deliberate practice to facilitate therapist development.

Ethics in Action: Innovating Ethics in the Counselling Professions

Series Editors:
Professor Lynne Gabriel and Professor Andrew Reeves

Series Description:

Ethical relating and working are at the core of the counselling professions. This series provides pragmatic resources in ethics for practitioners in the psychological professions, including counsellors, psychotherapists, counselling psychologists, practitioner trainers, supervisors and researchers; both trainee and trained. The books feature accessible and pragmatic resources on ethics in applied practice across a range of counselling and therapeutic contexts that will assist readers in decision-making in daily practice. The series aims to support meaning-making and ethical decision-making, providing responses for practitioners to key practice questions including "so what does this mean in practice for me, working in this context, with this client group?"

Books in Series:

Navigating Relational Ethics in Day-to-Day Practice: Working Ethically in the Counselling Professions
by Lynne Gabriel and Andrew Reeves

Relational Ethics in Psychotherapy and Counselling Private Practice: Solidarity, Compassion, Justice
by Caz Binstead and Nicholas Sarantakis

Ethics in Participatory Research on Counselling and Psychotherapy: Justice, Solidarity and Care
by John McLeod and Julia McLeod

Ethics in Participatory Research on Counselling and Psychotherapy

Justice, Solidarity and Care

John McLeod
Julia McLeod

Routledge
Taylor & Francis Group
LONDON AND NEW YORK

Designed cover image: © Getty Images

First published 2025
by Routledge
4 Park Square, Milton Park, Abingdon, Oxon OX14 4RN

and by Routledge
605 Third Avenue, New York, NY 10158

Routledge is an imprint of the Taylor & Francis Group, an informa business

© 2025 John McLeod and Julia McLeod

The right of John McLeod and Julia McLeod to be identified as authors of this work has been asserted in accordance with sections 77 and 78 of the Copyright, Designs and Patents Act 1988.

All rights reserved. No part of this book may be reprinted or reproduced or utilised in any form or by any electronic, mechanical, or other means, now known or hereafter invented, including photocopying and recording, or in any information storage or retrieval system, without permission in writing from the publishers.

Trademark notice: Product or corporate names may be trademarks or registered trademarks, and are used only for identification and explanation without intent to infringe.

British Library Cataloguing-in-Publication Data
A catalogue record for this book is available from the British Library

ISBN: 9781032522630 (hbk)
ISBN: 9781032522616 (pbk)
ISBN: 9781003405818 (ebk)

DOI: 10.4324/9781003405818

Typeset in Times New Roman
by codeMantra

For Eva, Isaac, Ella and Gracie

Contents

Acknowledgements

We would like to acknowledge the help and support we have received, in relation to the issues explored in this book, from Sophia Balamoutsou, Nicola Blunden, David Denborough, Elise Ferguson, Lynne Gabriel, Lisa Goodman, Christine Kupfer, Thomas Mackrill, Marie-Clare Murphie, Andrew Reeves, Alison Rouse, Kate Smith, Fiona Stirling, Rolf Sundet, Mhairi Thurston, Marius Veseth, Dot Weaks, Heather Wilkinson, and Marguerite Woods. Our deepest thanks also go to our editorial and production team at Routledge: Grace McDonnell, Prisha Revar, Kris Šiošytė.

Introduction

This book explores the moral and ethical dimensions of participatory research in counselling and psychotherapy. An appreciation of ethical issues is fundamentally important for anyone undertaking participatory research because, at its heart, this kind of study seeks to challenge injustice by giving equal (or more) weight to the life experience and cultural knowledge of ordinary people in situations in which service provision and models of care have previously been largely controlled by professional elites. It is inevitable, in all participatory research studies, that dilemmas and tensions associated with differences in power and knowledge are played out in the research process. To be able to carry out a participatory study, therefore, it is not enough to possess technical skills around research design, data collection, and analysis. This kind of work also requires a capacity to handle difficult ethical choices and relationships on a day-to-day basis, and an appreciation of how general principles (justice, solidarity, and care) play out in specific situations.

While participatory research methods have been widely adopted in fields such as education, healthcare, management studies, and community development, it has been used much less frequently in therapy research. Participatory research can only be adequately appreciated through seeing how it works in particular contexts. The book therefore offers a wide range of examples of participatory research in therapy that illustrate different ways that a participatory approach has been implemented in relation to different research questions.

There has been a massive expansion of interest and activity in participatory research, and similar methodologies, in the recent years. While it is not feasible to offer comprehensive coverage of that literature in a book of this length, the intention has been to include sufficient sources to allow the reader points of contact with the key strands of work being pursued in this area.

A fundamental aspect of participatory research is that it requires a willingness to move beyond defining an area of practice, such as counselling, psychotherapy, or life coaching, solely or predominantly in terms of the assumptions, interests, and purposes of professionals (practitioners and researchers). Participatory research inevitably broadens the focus of an investigation, in the direction of taking account of what that

DOI: 10.4324/9781003405818-1

aspect of social life looks like from the perspective of service users, clients, carers, and members of the public, in general. A valuable aspect of participatory research on therapy is that it encompasses not only what happens in therapy sessions, but also the much broader set of ways that ordinary people engage in psychotherapeutic activities, and make sense of these experiences, in their everyday lives.

An important aim of this book is to inform those who have a stake or interest in psychotherapeutic processes, but are not professional therapists or researchers, around how involvement in participatory research might be meaningful and beneficial to them.

Chapter 1 explores the development of participatory research, different forms that this approach can take, and how it has been applied to topics in the field of counselling and psychotherapy. Chapter 2 looks at how a participatory approach to research engages with moral issues around injustice and adversity, and building relationships around principles of solidarity and care. Chapters 3–8 focus on a series of ethical themes: social justice, power and privilege, relationships, respect for diversity, personal challenges, and courage. Chapter 9 returns to what – for most readers – is the underlying reason for doing research at all, which is the intention to learn how to do better therapy, and reflects on the implications of participatory research for therapy practice.

Each chapter concludes with a set of topics for reflection and discussion. These questions are primarily intended to facilitate deeper personal engagement with ideas introduced in the chapter. It can also be valuable to discuss one's response to a topic with a small group of learning partners, to gain an appreciation of other perspectives around each issue. Topics may also be relevant for tutors, in terms of essay and seminar titles.

The issues discussed in this book, and the types of study that are described, are applicable to all therapy approaches. Participatory research is not associated with any particular model of therapy or therapy modality (e.g., one-to-one, couples/family therapy, group therapy).

This book does not claim to provide a comprehensive handbook of participatory research in therapy. Instead, we have tried to offer a straightforward introduction, with short focused chapters supported by vivid examples, learning activities, and suggestions for further reading. We hope that what we have written will be helpful for students at an early stage in their research careers, more experienced researchers who are contemplating carrying out a participatory research study, and all those who are taking part in such studies. It should also be of value for those who are interested in reading participatory studies and want to develop a better appreciation of the strengths and limitations of this approach. While the examples provided in the book are mainly grounded in counselling and psychotherapy studies, the kinds of issues being discussed should be recognisable and relevant to those with a background in other areas of applied psychology, as well as in mental health, social work, and similar fields.

Chapter 1

Participatory research on counselling and psychotherapy

A brief introduction

Introduction

Counselling and psychotherapy are highly complex activities. To respond to the concerns and unique life circumstances of clients, a therapist needs to be able to draw on an array of sources of knowledge including the life experience and accumulated wisdom and experience of both the client and themselves, ideas that exist within their community and culture around helping and healing, and theories of therapy. Knowledge from scientific research has the potential to make a distinctive and significant contribution to therapy practice, on the basis of offering evidence that is grounded in a process of systematic, rigorous, and critical inquiry and debate within a global scientific community.

Over the past 50 years, a major achievement of the counselling and psychotherapy research community has been an appreciation that making sense of the process and outcome of therapy requires the development and application of many different approaches to inquiry. The therapy literature comprises studies that use qualitative, quantitative, and mixed methods; big data sets; intensive analysis of single cases; controlled clinical trials; exploratory studies; theory-building studies; objective measurement; and personal experience studies (autoethnography).

However, despite the productivity and ingenuity of several generations of therapy researchers, it is apparent that there has been something missing in the way that research has been understood and carried out. Surveys and interviews with front-line therapy practitioners, on their attitude to research and use of research knowledge, have consistently shown that, while they accept in principle that research is necessary, they seldom read research articles, and believe that researchers are asking the wrong questions. At a societal level, policy decisions made by government health departments around which types of therapy services should be offered, have been made on the basis of evidence from research studies that have investigated which therapy approaches are most effective for specific client problems. However, in many instances these policies have been met with large-scale resistance from clients, practitioners, and other stakeholders, on the grounds that what is provided is not sufficiently sensitive to the needs, preferences, and cultural beliefs of service

DOI: 10.4324/9781003405818-2

users and their communities (see, for example, McPherson, 2020; McPherson and Beresford, 2019).

Therapy research has generated a massively expanded insight and understanding around what happens in the therapy room, and the helpfulness (or otherwise) of different processes and interventions. It has contributed to the credibility of counselling and psychotherapy, as professions that are willing to look openly and critically at their practices. It has given governments and health insurance companies confidence that investing in therapy is justifiable. But, so far, it has not made a great deal of difference to the quality of the therapy experience of clients. A client seeing a therapist today would be no more likely to be satisfied with what they had received, than a client seeing a therapist in the 1960s. And also, as a rule, the people who receive therapy are still from the same social backgrounds.

Taken together, these observations suggest that while particular pieces of therapy research may be interesting, and even inspiring, there remain major questions around how *useful* it is, as a whole, in relation to informing policy and practice (McLeod, 2016).

There are many reasons why therapy research has not translated into a reduction in emotional pain and suffering at a societal level. Much suffering is driven by social and political factors (racism, colonialism, gender violence, social class inequalities, etc.) that are beyond the remit of therapy. It is also important to acknowledge that the therapy research community itself is fragmented by the strong dividing lines that exist between therapy approaches (McLeod, 2017). Research groups affiliated to specific therapy traditions, such as CBT or psychoanalysis, tend to operate in isolation from each other. As a consequence, therapy researchers have struggled to establish the kind of industrial-scale knowledge networks that have underpinned the success of science in other areas of contemporary life (e.g., vaccines to protect against COVID-19).

Given the intrinsic limitations of both therapy as a means of addressing human suffering and mental health problems, and the capacities of the therapy research community, it is essential to make the best of the resources that we have. But, how can we make better use of the research techniques and methodologies that we have and the research workforce that is available? The answer to this is to work together, in ways that maximise the knowledge, understanding, and energies of *all* of those for whom therapy is a meaningful and significant part of their lives: clients, therapists, and other stakeholders such as carers, community groups, members of the public, and members of professions with overlapping interests. Rather than researchers and research teams conducting studies *on* clients and therapists, this involves a shift in the direction of research *with* them. Rather than research that is driven by the questions and ideas of academic researchers who are inevitably somewhat distanced from practice, all aspects of the research process reflect the standpoints of those who have knowledge *from* and *through* experience, and whose primary interest is in making a difference at a practical level.

Research that seeks to purposefully and systematically bring together the experience, skills, and knowledge of researchers and experts by experience has been in existence for many years. It has been described in many different ways: collaborative inquiry, action research, participative, feminist, Indigenous, service user, pluralistic, co-produced research, patient and public involvement, citizen science, engaged research, de-centred research, pluralistic inquiry. The common thread across all of these approaches is a commitment on the part of the researcher to facilitate the active and meaningful participation of individuals and groups from outside the university or research team. In the present book, we use the term 'participatory research' to refer to this rich tradition.

A key assumption in participatory research is that useful practical knowledge emerges through dialogue across perspectives and that an over-reliance on any single perspective (e.g., that of the researcher) will result in an unhelpful silencing of voices that have valuable insights to offer. Science has always advanced through lively debate and exchange of views, but this has almost entirely taken place within the scientific community itself. Participatory research can therefore be seen as an opening-out and democratisation of the kind of critical dialogical or dialectical process that has always represented a central aspect of science.

What is participatory research?

The term participatory research refers to a broad range of research approaches and traditions that – to a greater or lesser extent – actively and purposefully seek to involve people who are not professional researchers in the process of designing and conducting a study. The rationale for participatory research encompasses both methodological and socio-political dimensions. From a methodological perspective, knowledge that is grounded in only a researcher's perspective is likely to miss, or downplay, themes and insights that are available to those who have direct, ongoing, personal experience of a topic, such as practitioners, service users, and community members. In addition, dialogue between researchers and participants has the potential to challenge assumptions and generate deeper understanding. From a socio-political perspective, participatory research represents an explicit commitment to fight injustice, by ensuring that research does not operate as a means of oppressing marginalised groups and by embracing the intention that a research study should have direct benefits for all those who have contributed to it.

Participatory research has its origins in social and cultural contexts characterised by overt exploitation of particular social groups arising from colonialism. Key figures in the early development of participatory research include Orlando Fals Borda (1925–2008; Colombia), Marja-Liisa Swantz (born in 1926 in Finland, worked in Tanzania), Paulo Freire (1921–1997; Brazil), and Rajesh Tandon (born in 1951; India). Participatory research emerged as a form of resistance to systems of government and colonialist-capitalist exploitation in situations where communities already possessed a legacy, or ongoing tradition, of local management of social life, underpinned by an Indigenous philosophical and moral stance that emphasised interdependence, mutual support, spirituality, and a sense of being part of a more-than-human world that sustained all life. Participatory research represented a means of maintaining and affirming these values while engaging with the requirement of government departments for evidence, fundable programmes, and project evaluation. From the start, participatory research was associated with organisations and academic disciplines in such field as education, economic development, and human rights. Although the promotion of individual well-being and group solidarity were implicit aims of participatory research, there was little explicit reference to ideas from psychology or psychotherapy.

From the 1980s, the relevance of participatory research began to be increasingly recognised in the Global North, for example, in relation to the development of services in fields such as health, social care, and community education, and in the area of organisational development (Cornwall & Jewkes, 1995). As well as drawing on the ideas of writers such as Paulo Freire and others mentioned above, these developments were also influenced by philosophical perspectives around the nature of knowledge offered by John Macmurray, Richard Rorty, John Dewey, and others, who promoted the notion that true knowing is inextricably linked with action. Many contemporary participatory action researchers also take inspiration from critical theory, developed by Jurgen Habermas and others, and feminist and liberationist approaches, around the argument that practical knowing necessarily involves a willingness and capacity to critically analyse the structures of power that operate within social systems, and explicitly to align the researcher with those who lack power, as a way of facilitating progressive change (Erikainen et al., 2021).

The existence of different styles of participatory research, appropriate to a diversity of settings, contexts, and purposes, has led to an ever-expanding list of methodological approaches: action research, appreciative inquiry, collaborative inquiry, co-produced research, group autoethnography, emancipatory research, feminist inquiry, decolonised inquiry, citizen science, mad studies, and service user research. Useful entry points into this complex methodological landscape include Bradbury (2015) and Chevalier and Buckles (2019). It is possible to identify a set of key principles that are shared by all forms of participative research:

- Power, decision-making, and responsibility are shared between professional researchers and other participants.
- The aim of a participatory research project is to contribute to improving the lives of participants and their community.
- Acknowledgement of pluralism: there are always multiple perspectives or standpoints in relation to any issue.
- Openness to whatever research techniques and methods are appropriate in the specific circumstances of a particular project, and to improvising data collection and analysis procedures; the validity of a study is not determined by the application of a fixed, pre-determined methodology.
- The outcomes and findings of research are disseminated in ways that support the social justice aims of the study – which may or may not involve publication of conventional academic papers.

The implementation of these principles calls for active and ongoing attention to issues around ethics and morality. For example, participatory research is driven by an intention to overcome injustice and support respectful and inclusive ways through which people can live together. The process of conducting a participatory research study requires building relationships between people who may have quite different backgrounds, goals, values, and skills. These core elements of participatory research call for a capacity to reflect on, and talk about, such matters as how co-researchers handle differences in power, manage disagreements and conflict within a research team, and learn to trust each other. This is a form of research that often has the potential to have a transformative effect on the lives of those who are involved. The literature on participatory research includes many sources that offer an expanded appreciation of the meaning of research ethics.

The extent and type of non-researcher involvement in a study can take many forms, depending on the context and research aims. Banks and Brydon-Miller (2019) suggest that it can be helpful to view participative research as existing on a continuum of degrees of participation. At one end of the continuum are studies that are entirely initiated, controlled, and managed by non-researchers, for example, by a community group or counselling service. At the next step along this continuum are studies that are community or service-lead, where professional researchers or research students are employed or contracted to work on their behalf. A major category of participatory research comprises a middle ground in which there is a partnership between researchers and non-researchers, reflecting an intention to jointly co-produce all aspects of the study. At the more researcher-controlled end of the continuum are studies that are directed by a researcher or university research team, where participants are nevertheless able to exert a meaningful degree of influence by advising on the design of a study, deciding on the questions in an interview schedule or questionnaire, carrying out interviews or distributing questionnaires, analysing data, writing the final report or research paper, and disseminating findings (e.g., organising events, giving talks, making podcasts, etc.). Some researcher-led studies may also comprise intensive personal participation through the use of data collection techniques such as keeping a diary or taking photographs of meaningful places within one's life space. A further category of participative research occurs in group or collective autoethnographic or writing projects, in which a set of people work together to reflect on, and analyse, their personal experience around a particular topic or question.

Because participatory research takes place in a range of community and institutional settings, the non-academic participants in a study are described using a wide array of labels that reflect terminology that makes sense in the specific context within which the study was carried out: participant, client, patient, consumer, adviser, representative, leader (e.g., youth leader), citizen, expert by experience, experiential expert, co-researcher.

How participatory research makes a distinctive contribution to practical knowledge

There is a broad consensus that, in relation to the kinds of complex issues investigated in research into health, social care, and other practice domains, all existing methodologies and ways of generating knowledge are in principle likely to be relevant. Most programmes of research around major topics tend to encompass the use of different methodologies, and different mixed methods research designs, at different phases, or in respect of different questions. It is therefore important to be able to identify the distinctive strengths and limitations of each research approach. Areas in which participatory methods may make a notable contribution include the following:

- Much mainstream research serves the interests of the powerful. By contrast, participatory research is based on a political stance of supporting marginalised, oppressed, and silenced individuals and communities.
- Action orientation: directly making a practical difference to people's lives (rather than accumulating abstract knowledge in libraries).
- People whose voices are typically excluded from research studies have important things to say (insider knowledge, knowledge-through-experience) that are not available to academic researchers: including such individuals as co-researchers has the potential to produce more objective, fine-grained, creative, and reality-based findings. Research that involves people with lived personal experience of the issue being investigated reduces the possibility of errors arising from academic researchers imposing their own assumptions and theories on data that are collected.
- Meaningful engagement in research, particularly in groups and communities that may be suspicious of the researcher's motives, Potential participants are more likely to sign up for a research project, and commit their time and effort, if they can see that members of their community, who they can identify with, have been involved in the design of a study.
- Practical knowledge arises from dialogue across/between perspectives: a participatory research study creates a situation in which people with different perspectives (or stories to tell) listen to each other and try to develop a shared perspective, thus expanding the horizon of understanding of all who are involved (Hersted et al., 2019).

Potential limitations of participatory research are that there are many research situations where it may not be possible to convene an advisory or co-production group. It may take more time to complete a study, compared to other approaches – additional meetings may be required to integrate the suggestions of community participants and to provide them with appropriate induction and training.

Learning about participatory research: further reading

Suggestions about key sources of information that can be of value for anyone undertaking participatory research are offered below.

An introductory overview of participatory research has been published by Liamputtong and Rice (2021). Practical guidelines and resources to support this kind of research can be found at Goodman, Thomas et al. (2017, 2018; www.cbprtoolkit.org) and Warwick-Booth et al. (2021; https://bristoluniversitypress.co.uk/creating-participatory-research-website). Detailed accounts of how specific (large-scale) participatory research projects were carried out, and lessons learned, are available in Katz-Wise et al. (2019) and Oaks et al. (2019).

Within the UK National Health Service, the National Institute for Health and Care Research (2021) has published detailed briefing notes for researchers undertaking participatory and public involvement studies in the field of health and social care research. In the field of co-produced, participatory research on mental health issues, led by service users, the McPin Foundation has been responsible for a substantial body of studies that exemplify a wide range of transformative forms of methodological innovation: https://mcpin.org.

An issue that has been identified within the participatory research literature is that studies do not report information about the involvement of service users and members of the public in a consistent manner. The Guidance for Reporting Involvement of Patients and the Public (GRIPP) checklist was developed to address this dilemma (Staniszewska et al., 2017). An example of how to report public/service user involvement in a participatory study can be found in the Abstract ('public involvement') and 'Limitations and Future Directions' sections in Bennett et al. (2022).

In terms of understanding how a participatory approach can emerge and build within a particular area of health and social care, it can be valuable to consider the example of collaborative research on dementia. Beyond the relevance of this topic for practitioners working in the field of dementia or mental health in older people, understanding the experience of living with dementia is relevant for anyone involved in psychotherapeutic practice, because they may have clients suffering from dementia, or carers. More broadly, the issues associated with coming to terms with a diagnosis of dementia, negotiating care, and dealing with social attitudes are similar in many ways to the challenges faced by other people who are living with a disability, long-term health condition, or other form of social adversity. Historically, research on dementia was conducted from a medical or psychiatric perspective in which the person with dementia was treated as an object of inquiry. From the 1970s, there began to emerge a political movement that sought to humanise dementia care, which began to be reflected in qualitative interview-based studies that sought to give people with dementia a voice. By the 1990s this shift led to an appreciation that it could be valuable to enlist people with dementia as active participants and co-researchers, who were able to influence the type of research questions that were pursued, and how data were collected, and analysed, and how findings were disseminated (Wilkinson, 2001). An important element of the literature at this stage was the increasing visibility of people with dementia as authors of published articles (e.g., McKillop & Wilkinson, 2004). A further landmark was the creation, by a combined service user and researcher group, of an accessible and straightforward set of practical guidelines for participatory research that involved people with dementia (Scottish Dementia Working Group Research Sub-Group, 2014). In turn, these guidelines created a platform that empowered groups of people to engage in participatory studies, and share what they had learned about how to undertake this type of work (for example, Mann & Hung, 2019; Murphy et al., 2015; Novek & Wilkinson, 2019; Swarbrick et al., 2019).

The story of the development of participatory research in dementia illustrates how local projects can link up over time to establish a shared framework for research practice that makes it easier for new researchers and service users to enter the field. For the pioneer researchers and patient advocates in this area, it was hard to get approval for participatory studies or to know how to carry out such a study once it had been approved. Gradually, however, a body of shared knowledge and experience became available. A further significant aspect of this story is that it illustrates how ethical principles around such themes as care, solidarity, and justice permeated all of these initiatives, and, in fact, can be seen as constant underlying factors that drove it forward.

The socio-political context of participatory research

The tension between top-down, institutionally controlled forms of knowing (such as mainstream science) and open systems of knowing that are grounded in collective action (such as participatory research) needs to be understood as one element of a much broader tension within human history. It is widely believed that human progress necessarily involves an inevitable movement from the kind of non-hierarchical form of organisation exemplified in hunter-gatherer tribes, to the largely centralised, State-controlled and bureaucratic style that prevails at the present time. However, a comprehensive analysis of historical evidence, conducted by Graeber and Wengrow (2021) found, instead, that cultures and societies have tended to move back and forward between centralised control and local autonomy, in responses to a wide range of factors. At the present time, although centralised decision-making, knowledge production, and education are dominant, there are also many examples of live traditions of collective action, in such areas as democratic participation (Russell, 2020), learning (Lave & Wenger, 1991), and the commons (Ostrom, 1990). A discussion of the implications of this perspective for therapy practice can be found in McLeod and Sundet (2022). What all this means, in relation to participatory research, is that although research into health and social care is largely dictated by expert-driven research and knowledge production, there remains a sufficient appreciation within ordinary people of the merits of a more collectivist approach. Dreyer et al. (2021) conducted a large-scale study in several European countries, around citizens' views regarding public engagement with research. What they found was that there existed a high level of appreciation of the value of active and detailed public involvement in research. Such attitudes are also apparent at a global level. A survey of young people aged 15–29 across five low- and middle-income countries (Nigeria, Brazil, Jamaica, South Africa, and Burundi) found that the majority were interested in contributing to mental health and well-being research (Pavarini et al., 2023). Focusing more closely on the attitudes of people with lived experience of mental health challenges to research involvement, McEvoy et al. (2023) found that individuals from such backgrounds appreciated the importance of such initiatives and were keen to take part while being realistic about the challenges that might they need to face if they did so.

Participatory research on psychotherapeutic practice

Until recently, and despite persuasive arguments on its behalf presented by Kidd and Kral (2005), participatory approaches have not been widely used in research on counselling and psychotherapy (Rodriguez Espinosa & Verney, 2021). We believe that participatory research has the potential to make a distinctive and significant contribution to enhancing the relevance and helpfulness of counselling, psychotherapy, and allied practice. The aim of the present book is to encourage and support more academic therapy researchers, students, practitioner-researchers, and community organisations to engage with this approach.

The absence of participatory research around therapy issues is illustrated by the findings of a study by Kennedy et al. (2022), who analysed the research approach used in more than 100 studies on the experiences of adult survivors of childhood abuse that had been published in the UK were subsequently assessed for level of participatory involvement. Within this set of studies, only 13% reported the active involvement (i.e., beyond being interviewed or completing a questionnaire) of abuse survivors. Even in those studies that did make use of participation by experts-by-experience, the most usual pattern was to invite a limited degree of consultation on a specific aspect of the study (e.g., formulating interview questions). There were very few survivor-led studies or examples of collaborative partnership between survivors and academic researchers.

A study by McPherson et al. (2020) illustrates the other side of the pattern of predominantly expert-controlled research described by Kennedy et al. (2022). McPherson et al. (2020) invited a group of non-researchers with an interest in therapy (clients, carers, GPs, mental health service managers) to attend a presentation on the methods and findings of a randomised controlled study of therapy for depression, and then meet in small groups to discuss their reactions to what they had heard. These individuals were highly critical and sceptical about all aspects of the study described to them. In particular, they identified many points at which the team that had carried out the depression seemed to be almost wilfully ignoring aspects of the experience of depression, and the process of therapy, that were obvious to anyone who had first-hand knowledge of these phenomena.

Why does so little therapy-related research make use of participatory methodology? One of the reasons for this has been that therapy research has been largely undertaken by psychologists and psychiatrists who have been trained in the predominantly quantitative, experimental, objective, and theoretically driven methodological traditions that have dominated research and inquiry in these disciplines. Although important strands of participatory research on psychological topics can be found in the work of the social psychologist Kurt Lewin in the 1940s, and the programme of organisational research based at the Tavistock Institute during the 1950s and 1960s, psychological research has tended to view the people who they study as passive 'subjects' rather than as 'participants' or 'co-researchers' with their own ideas and purposes.

It is only within the last 20 years that there has been a broadening-out of research in psychology and psychotherapy, in the direction of allowing space for qualitative, autoethnographic, critical, feminist, and participatory research approaches.

A further reason for the lack of participatory research in the field of counselling and psychotherapy is that the role of the researcher and that of the participant inevitably intersects in complex ways. For example, many therapy researchers have been, or continue to be, either (or both) clients and therapists. As a means of handling these overlapping identities, it is possible that therapy researchers have chosen to create strong boundaries between them. It is also possible that, because they have their own first-hand knowledge of therapy, they believe they have no further need to involve experts by experience.

It may also be the case that therapy researchers do not wish to open themselves up to challenges from research participants who question their assumptions about therapy, and are on the whole not interested in how inequalities of power, status, and control influence therapy practice, and research. Adopting a participatory approach changes the focus of counselling and psychotherapy research. Kidd and Krall (2005) described participatory methods as requiring a shift in attitude in the direction of sharing power, and greater willingness to be involved in everyday struggles experienced by members of a community.

A participatory research orientation is grounded in a pluralistic standpoint that acknowledges there are always multiple perspectives that exist in relation to any aspect of how people live their lives, and multiple ways in which problems in living can be tackled. In other words, therapy is not just something that is done by therapists, but also involves what clients (or people in general) do to tackle life difficulties, and the ways they adapt or modify therapy ideas and activities in these endeavours. The implications of this kind of pluralistic stance for research into counselling, psychotherapy, and allied practices are discussed by Smith et al. (2021). In the context of the present book, these considerations are reflected in the use of the phrase 'psychotherapeutic practice', alongside terms such as counselling and psychotherapy. Psychotherapeutic practice encompasses not only formal counselling and psychotherapy delivered by a trained therapist, but also other relevant activities undertaken by people – instead of formal counselling and psychotherapy or alongside it – to cope with relational and emotional problems and living.

To provide a sense of what participatory research looks like in relation to psychotherapeutic practice, examples of therapy studies that have utilised different ways of making use of participation by non-researchers are outlined below. Further examples can be found in the McPin Foundation website, as well as in McLeod (2011; chapter 11), and later chapters of the present book.

Research conducted entirely by non-researchers. There is nothing to prevent anyone from carrying out a study of therapy. In other areas of science, such as ecology, there exists a strong tradition of citizen science. Similarly, within the world of therapy and mental health, important contributions to knowledge have been made by individuals operating entirely independently of the academic system. A particularly successful and influential example of this type of work was a study carried out by the American writer and journalist Deborah Lott (2000), into the experiences of women clients around their relationships with their therapists.

Projects initiated and managed by community groups who employ professional researchers. Belfast. There have been many research studies and reports on therapy topics that have been produced by service user organisations. In a UK context, examples of such projects can be found on the websites of the mental health charity MIND (www.mind.org.uk) and the depression charity AWARE (https://aware-ni.org). Although these organisations either employed or commissioned academic researchers, the agency itself largely controls the research aims and process, and the way that findings are reported. An example of this form of participatory research is a large-scale study of barriers to access to talking therapies, produced by a group of UK charities (MIND, 2013). McConnell et al. (2018) analysed the experience of participatory research within AWARE.

Using a client/service user advisory group. In some studies, an advisory group, comprising individuals with lived experience of the topic being investigated, is involved in all aspects of a study. In many situations, a time-limited group is established for the purposes of a specific project. An example of this approach can be found in a study by Spong and Waters (2015) and Waters et al. (2018) into the attitudes of carers around the value of counselling to help them cope with the demands of their caring role. In this study, a group of counselling researchers invited members of a local carer organisation to advise and be directly involved in many aspects of the study, including its design, formulation of interview questions, recruiting interviewees, and analysis of interview data. Smith et al. (2021) invited members of an advisory group to be involved in the analysis of interviews that had been carried out with mental health service users around their recovery journey. In universities and research centres where there is an ongoing commitment to participatory inquiry, a permanent advisory group or collaboration agreement may be set up, to provide an independent perspective on a series of projects. An example of a permanent advisory group is the Service User Research Enterprise (SURE) (https://www.kcl.ac.uk/research/sure) at Kings College London, which consists of survivors of different types of trauma and mental health intervention. A recent project by this group was a programme of participatory research into improving therapy assessment for trauma survivors. This consisted of survivor-led qualitative interviews of undergoing psychotherapy assessment (Faulkner et al., 2023), co-produced systematic reviews of previous research on this topic (Patel et al., 2022; Sweeney et al. 2019), and a co-produced consultation exercise around the practical implications of these findings (Sweeney et al., 2022). Key practical outputs from this programme included a set of trauma-informed assessment guidelines for therapists and therapy provider organisations (Sweeney, 2021) and a paper outlining a rationale for the significance and implementation of these recommendations (Sweeney & Taggart, 2018). A further example of the involvement of a longstanding advisory group consisting of service users can be found in a series of studies in Norway, largely focused on therapeutic support for individuals diagnosed with bipolar personality disorder (Veseth et al., 2016, 2017). An advisory group structure has also been established at Oxford University (Oxford Neuroscience, Ethics and Society Young People's Advisory Group; NeurOx YPAG) to support research into ethical aspects of the use of new technologies to address mental health issues in young people (Pavarini et al., 2019). An example of the kind of work being undertaken by this group is a study of online help-seeking, largely carried out by 10 co-researchers aged 14–18 years (Bennett et al., 2022). Bacha et al. (2020) used the management committee of a service user organisation as an advisory group, in a study of user experiences of therapeutic relationships.

Studies initiated and managed by academic researchers, in which participants function as co-researchers. In some instances, adopting a participatory approach has been accomplished by giving informants, for instance, people who have been interviewed around their experience of an issue, the option of contributing to other stages of the research process. In a study of recovery strategies in women who had survived childhood sexual abuse, Morrow and Smith (1995) first of all interviewed women who had agreed to be part of the study, and then invited them to join with the main researcher in group sessions that focused on analysing the interview data. Further reflective reports on what this process was like, for all concerned, were subsequently published by Morrow (2006, 2009). Matheson and Weightman (2021a) invited patients who had completed therapy in an NHS clinic in London, to become co-researchers in a study of their experiences of psychotherapy for complex post-traumatic stress disorder. These co-researchers were involved in designing the interview schedule, conducting interviews, and analysing data. Matheson and Weightman (2021b) also collected information about how participation in this project had supported the process of recovery for these individuals. Knowles et al. (2022) describe a co-design process to inform a systematic review of outcomes of interventions to support young people struggling with issues of self-harm. Working with youth organisations, they engaged in an iterative inquiry procedure with successive groups of young people, to elicit their ideas about key questions and issues that they believed should be addressed in the review. Service user involvement in systematic review projects are discussed by Pollock et al. (2019). Within the "What's Up With Everyone?" project, Ito-Jaeger et al. (2022) involved young people in a process of developing animations to promote mental health literacy, and then analysing their effectiveness. Participatory studies that are led by academic researchers typically include initiatives to train service user participants in research skills and awareness (Blair et al., 2022; Desai et al, 2019).

Studies where everyone involved is both a researcher and participant. Participatory research can take the form of a highly reflexive and collective style of inquiry, in which all those involved are engaged in both contributing information about their personal experience of a topic or phenomenon, and then analysing it. One way of undertaking this kind of study is through the use of group or collective autoethnography. In a study of the meaning of personal therapy for psychotherapists, a group of six therapists took turns to write about their experience and then discuss these accounts in a group (Råbu et al., 2021). Notes from each group meeting were then fed back into the cycle of inquiry. In the final phase of this project, the group turned towards identifying shared themes across their individual stories, and jointly writing a paper for publication. A similar approach was used in a study conducted by a group of counselling psychology doctoral students, in relation to their experiences of authenticity in their training and practice (Yang et al., 2023), and a study of self-harm by Stirling and Chandler (2021). In a collaborative action research study, Davies and Morris (2018) engaged in an extended mutual inquiry process around the meaning of gender in their therapy practice. In Beck et al. (2005), a group consisting of both senior therapists and trainees engaged in a collective phenomenological inquiry into their experience of despair in the therapy process. West (1996, 1997) used collaborative inquiry groups to enable therapists to explore and document their experiences of integrating spirituality into their practice.

De-centred research. The community of therapists and community activists associated with narrative therapy have developed a distinctive type of action-oriented participatory research in which the researcher is a facilitator who supports one group or community to document their stories of resilience and survival in a form that can make a difference to other groups or communities faced with similar challenges (Denborough, 2011, 2012). In one such project, Denborough et al. (2006) assisted members of an Aboriginal community to create a list of their special skills for responding to losses, and then worked with a different community around the implications of that list for them, and their reply to it. Other examples of de-centred narrative inquiry include Gaddis (2004), Pastor (2020), and Tootell (2004).

Practice Research Networks. A PRN (Practice Research Network or Practitioner Research Network) consists of a collaborative arrangement between academic researchers and front-line counsellors or psychotherapists, with the aim of carrying out research that is relevant to practice. Typically, this involves meetings to agree on research priorities and questions, leading to data being collected by therapists in the context of their routine practice, that are then discussed, analysed, and written up by the group as a whole (Barkham, 2014). PRNs have been established within particular approaches to therapy practice (e.g., art therapy), or organised around specific settings and client groups (e.g., student counselling). It requires considerable skill, resilience, and commitment to maintain such relationships over the course of a project (Youn et al., 2019). Practitioners generally report that involvement in a PRN is meaningful and worthwhile, but hard to integrate into other work demands (Castonguay et al. (2010). Examples of studies carried out by a PRN are an exploration of therapist experiences of moments in therapy when there emerges an intense sense of meeting and connection between therapist and client (Harris et al., 2020), and an investigation of the impact of relationship skills training on quality of working alliance (Tasca et al., 2023). Other studies arising from the work of various PRNs are summarised in Castonguay et al. (2021). A notably successful PRN has been the group within the British Association for Art Therapists (BAT), which was set up in 2000 (Huet et al., 2014), with the aim of supporting multiple studies carried out by different individuals in groups, rather than focusing on a single project (Springham & Xenophontes, 2021).

Participatory development of therapy measures. Self-report questionnaires and rating scales that measure aspects of the process and outcome of therapy have made a massive contribution to the advancement of knowledge about therapy. Until recently, such measures were entirely conceived and designed by academic researchers, with minimal input from clients. A significant development within the broad shift in the direction of service user participation in mental health policy and decision-making has been a growing body of evidence that many clients and service users do not regard widely used outcome and process measures to be relevant to their experiences and needs (Crawford et al., 2011). This realisation has resulted in many initiatives that have involved user participation in measure design and development (Carlton et al., 2020; Rose et al., 2011). For example, the organisation that operates KOOTH (www.kooth.com), an online counselling and mental health resource for young people, wanted to develop an outcome measure that would be acceptable and relevant to their client group and could be routinely used to evaluate the effectiveness of their service. This project involved two stages. First, an extensive consultation exercise was carried out with counsellors employed by KOOTH, to generate a model of the kinds of goals and change processes that they observed in their clients (Hanley et al., 2021). Then, young people were involved in transforming these ideas into a set of questions that would make sense to clients (de Ossorno Garcia et al., 2021). Other areas in which participatory approach has been used to develop measures designed by service users include counselling and support for young people (Barbic et al., 2022; Perry et al., 2016), inpatient care (Evans et al., 2012), depression experience of Black men (Adams et al., 2021), and various aspects of recovery (Connell et al., 2018; Keetharuth et al., 2018; Marino, 2015; Neale et al., 2015).

Participatory involvement in the design and implementation of controlled outcome studies. Controlled outcome studies, such as randomised trials that compare the effectiveness of different therapy interventions, represent a highly influential source of evidence in relation to policy-making around service provision. One of the limitations of this type of research is that many clients, therapists, and community members regard it as generating an over-simplified, and therefore misleading, picture of the effectiveness of therapy (McPherson et al., 2020. In response, some therapy researchers have started to experiment with different ways of introducing a greater degree of client and therapist participation in the design and implementation of such studies. Ejbye-Ernst and Jorring (2017) describe how they used a participatory inquiry process to address resistance to controlled outcome research in therapists and clients within a narrative family therapy clinic in Denmark, through a process of co-designing a study that would be acceptable to them. McConnell et al. (2018) carried out a participatory research around how service users could be meaningfully involved in all aspects of a controlled outcome study in a community counselling and support service for depressed people in Northern Ireland. Goldsmith et al. (2019) present a detailed analysis of service user involvement in co-design around the planning of a randomised controlled trial study of mental health peer support.

Conclusions

Participatory research represents an important approach to the generation of practical knowledge that is increasingly used in fields such as health and social care. A range of styles of participatory research have been implemented in studies of counselling, psychotherapy, and broader mental health and psychotherapeutic topics. There have been relatively few substantial and sustained programmes of research that have adopted this approach, and it has had a relatively limited impact within the psychotherapy research literature as a whole. Nevertheless, on the basis of the limited number of the participatory studies that have been conducted, in the field of counselling and psychotherapy that it is possible to adapt this kind of dialogical, community-based approach to knowledge production to generate new insights in respect of many different therapy topics and questions. Moving forward, there are many opportunities to build on and extend this first phase of participatory therapy research in creative ways.

Reflection on the kinds of topics explored in participatory studies of therapy shows that – just as with participatory research in health and social care – this methodology is particularly well-suited to research that has had the goal of addressing inequality and injustice. Participatory research in therapy has tended to focus on areas in which clients and therapists have felt that existing studies have not adequately represented their experiences and needs, or situations in which they have not been treated fairly or their voices have not been heard. The willingness, in any type of participatory research, for academic researchers and clients (or members of the public, or therapy practitioners) to work together to generate new understanding, is grounded in a sense of solidarity in relation to overcoming injustice. Undertaking this kind of research calls for a willingness to be open to learning from the experience of the other, and to be committed to working through differences. These are processes that require those who are involved in a study to care for, and be careful with, each other. To carry out participatory research, it is not sufficient to know about research design and methodology, engaging with the moral, ethical, and political dimensions of this type of study is also essential. These areas are explored in the following chapter.

Questions for reflection and discussion

The following topics may be explored individually, and/or with a group of learning partners.

1 Access, download, and read any one of the participatory studies cited in this chapter that describes an investigation of a counselling or psychotherapy topic, or a question that relates to the wider field of mental health, well-being, and psychotherapeutic activities. In what ways, and to what extent, did the participatory dimension of your chosen study make a positive contribution to the credibility and relevance of findings? In what ways could this dimension have functioned as a limiting factor that reduced the value of the study? When you look at other studies on the same

topic, did the participatory study generate findings and practice implications that went beyond those reported by more conventional studies?

2 Look at other studies (or one key study) – that have influenced your practice as a therapist, or your use of psychotherapeutic activities in your everyday life. Alternatively, reflect on a study that you have personally conducted, or are in the process of planning. How might the study/studies you have identified have been enhanced if a more participatory research approach been utilised? At what points in the study could a participatory or co-production element have been added, and how might this have been accomplished (i.e., what would the researcher need to have done)?
3 Choose one participatory study you have read. Imagine what it would have been like to have been a client, service user, citizen, or practitioner participant or co-production team member, in that study. What is your sense of what might have been the positive aspects of being a participant, and what might have been the more problematic aspects? In the paper you selected, how effectively did the author(s) report and reflect on these positive or problematic participant experiences?

Chapter 2

Pluralistic ethics for participatory research

Introduction

In the researcher-led type of study that predominates within the field of therapy research, ethical issues are mainly discussed in relation to safeguarding the confidentiality and well-being of research subjects, and the challenges arising from the need to obtain ethical approval from an Ethics Committee or Institutional Review Board (IRB). By contrast, participatory research involves creating a situation in which the researcher and other participants are partners in the research enterprise (co-researchers), and share responsibility for what happens. These aspects of participatory research require constant attention to issues of fairness, respect, and equality within the research process. In addition, an essential element of the rationale for participatory methodologies is their orientation towards promoting social justice. As a consequence of these factors, compared to traditional expert-driven research, participatory research has a broader ethical and moral agenda.

The aim of this chapter is to examine how attending to ethical issues associated with participatory research on therapy topics calls for a pluralistic approach that incorporates different ethical perspectives and draws on a range of skills and strategies.

Why ethics are important for therapy practice and research

The concepts of ethics and morality refer to the fundamental assumptions about what is good or bad, acceptable or unacceptable, within particular cultures and social groups at specific points in time. Moral beliefs, values and assumptions, and stories about virtuous or evil forms of behaviour represent powerful emotional ties that bind a community together. In all cultures, minor but forgivable moral transgressions lead to significant penalties that provide strong warnings that such behaviour is not acceptable. All cultures also provide pathways to redemption, rehabilitation and forgiveness, and sophisticated systems of reasoning for allocating degrees of culpability, responsibility, and blame. In addition, in all cultures, exclusion (and self-exclusion) from the group occurs if a moral violation cannot be healed.

DOI: 10.4324/9781003405818-3

Within both the deep history and early modern history of human civilisation, cultures, societies, and nations have been organised around moral codes that were constantly reinforced through collective ritual and storytelling within an oral culture. In the period since around 1700, these moral frameworks have gradually fragmented in the face of scientific rationalism, literacy (traditional story-based transmission of moral principles being replaced by written codes), dualistic modes of thinking, and the forced imposition of capitalist (i.e., extractive, profit-driven and consumerist values). At the same time, globalisation and the interpenetration of a diversity of moral belief systems into almost all cultures have resulted in growing levels of ethical uncertainty. To a large extent, shared moral rituals and narratives that support social cohesion have been replaced by transient fictional narratives (novels, movies) whose ethical message may be ambiguous or even morally toxic.

Despite these factors, on a day-to-day basis, most people continue to behave towards others with kindness and respect. Nevertheless, the degree of moral uncertainty and fragmentation that exists in contemporary society can often lead to individuals and families regularly encountering moral dilemmas that are hard to resolve.

Within contemporary society, there are several strategies that are available to individuals and social groups in respect of addressing moral dilemmas. One mechanism is fundamentalism – living in accordance with a strict and inflexible set of moral precepts. Another mechanism is democracy – open dialogue within a community or society, leading to compromise and mutual acceptance around ethical questions. Therapy offers a further approach to handling everyday moral and ethical issues: meeting with another person, or as a family or group, to engage in meaningful and reflective conversations with the aim of building a personal way of moving forward in relation to a moral choice or dilemma.

On the whole, therapy is not usually discussed from a moral perspective, other than in relation to the necessity for maintaining professional ethical standards around such matters as confidentiality and avoidance of harm to therapy clients and research participants. However, responding to moral issues represents a potentially hugely significant aspect of therapy practice.

Therapy as a moral arena

The counselling and psychotherapy literature rarely use moral concepts to describe or make sense of psychotherapeutic practice. People are described as seeking therapy because of conditions such as depression and anxiety, or in response to events such as bereavement or trauma. Therapy is understood as being helpful because it leads to changes in the person's sense of self, their social skills, and their capacity for rational reflective thinking, brain functioning, and ability to regulate emotions. Research into therapy, for the most part, focuses on analysing these processes and analysing or measuring the outcomes of therapy.

A closer look at what is actually happening in the lives of people who engage in psychotherapeutic activities suggests that most of them are troubled by experiences of moral injustice. A substantial proportion of what can be categorised as mental health problems in adult life can be linked to childhood adversity. The reality of childhood sources of adversity is that most of them refer to situations in which the child has been treated badly by other people – they have been sexually abused, subjected to violence, not cared for properly, lied to, and bullied. Emotional and behavioural difficulties and lack of a sense of self-worth can also arise from situations in which the person has been subjected to micro-aggressive statements and actions from others, which convey a message that they are not an acceptable member of society. Or they have been shamed for some aspect of their identity, such as being queer or being differently abled. Alongside these types of events, that can at least be remembered and talked about, are other morally problematic experiences that are so taken for granted that they seldom enter awareness: many of the things we own, or the food we eat, are the result of exploitation of animals and the natural environment.

In therapy sessions, clients consistently talk about situations in which they have felt betrayed, humiliated, degraded, lied to, had their human rights denied, or had their right to exist placed in question. Therapy clients tend to use the word "should" a lot, to indicate that there are "right" and "wrong" courses of action that may be taken, or choices that might be made, in relation to a situation. When seeking psychotherapeutic support, people tell stories about specific events that have troubled them (or sometimes stories that point towards a better future). Such stories always have an explicit or implied 'moral' in terms of what they convey in respect of right and wrong ways to think or act. The motivation to enter therapy can be seen as arising from the experience of being 'demoralised' (Frank, 1974). The beneficial effects of therapy can be understood as arising from a process of coming to terms with the effects of such moral injustices, leading to a sense of being 're-moralised' – a recovery of an energising faith in the underlying goodness of other people, oneself, and the world as a whole.

Participatory research as a commitment to social justice

All science and research are grounded in ethical values such as a commitment to truth, honest reporting of findings, the personal integrity of the researcher, and the belief that scientific knowledge has the potential to make a vital contribution to human progress and well-being. Participatory research takes these moral principles a step further, by arguing that the way that science operates, for instance, its requirement for substantial resources and funding, and its reliance of technical expertise and training and location within elite universities, has had the effect of losing sight of the substantial knowledge already possessed by ordinary people, and the legitimate interests of marginalised groups in society. As a consequence, participatory research operates within a set of ethical criteria regarding the alignment of a research study with broader social justice objectives. In relation to the actual conduct of a research study, a participatory approach depends on the existence of solidarity and care in relationships between professional researchers and those service users or community members who are participating as co-researchers.

Taken together, consideration of the underlying moral and ethical meaning and purpose of both therapy practice and research requires that anyone undertaking participatory therapy research needs to be able to draw on a rich repertoire of ways of making sense of such issues, and also a flexible capacity to use relevant ethical skills and strategies to handle specific situations that may arise.

Pluralistic ethics: multiple perspectives

The concept of pluralism refers to a philosophical standpoint that, in matters of significance for human beings, there do not exist single valid truths or perspectives. Instead, there are always multiple credible perspectives. Positive and life-enhancing periods within the history of human culture and society have been characterised not by rigid certainties, but by openness to learning based on dialogue and respect for different views. Healthy, tolerant pluralism is evident in many areas of contemporary culture, for instance, around an acceptance of different lifestyles, political and religious beliefs, and cultural traditions. By allowing space for many different theories and forms of practice, counselling and psychotherapy can be seen as profoundly pluralistic. The field of research as a whole is also highly pluralistic in its willingness to recognise the relevance of diverse methodologies.

It is important to emphasise that pluralism does not represent a form of 'anything goes' relativism or scepticism. Rather, mature pluralism assumes that individuals and social groups will always hold beliefs that, for them, are highly meaningful and true. A pluralistic stance reflects a 'both/and' position that looks for ways of building bridges between apparently conflicting, rather than getting locked into an 'either/or' scenario where one of right and the other is wrong (Johnson, 2017, 2024; Novis-Deutsch, 2020; Viney, 2022).

Ethical and moral awareness and a capacity to talk about such issues are necessary elements of any attempt to sustain a pluralistic worldview. If conflicts between different beliefs and lifestyles, or between different assumptions about what counts as evidence, are to be resolved in a respectful and democratic manner, both (or all) parties need to be able to find or create a meeting point of common humanity based on shared values.

In the context of participatory research, what this means is that operating in accordance with a fixed set of ethical rules is never going to be sufficient. There will always be situations in which one specific rule is contradicted by a different rule, or it is not clear whether a rule applies at all, or the participant is operating according to their own rules, or there are alternative interpretations around how a particular rule might apply. The point here is not that ethical rules are unnecessary. For example, an ethical stipulation typically made by research ethics committees is: 'participant personal information must be securely stored, must be redacted from data sets, and must be deleted within a certain period of time following completion of the study'. These are useful and sensible rules that offer clarity and reassurance to all those involved in a study. However, they are not sufficient for dealing with all situations in which access to participant personal information may be in question – researchers always need to be able to draw on a broader set of principles and values.

A pluralistic ethical stance is a way of thinking about ethics that suggests that it can be helpful to develop a broad understanding of a range of perspectives on ethical and moral issues. Being in possession of a repertoire of ethical perspectives and concepts makes it easier to be aware of ethical dilemmas, anticipate and prevent difficulties, and formulate constructive ways of responding to sticky situations. Dealing with ethical dilemmas and choices is always a relational and collaborative process – an appreciation of different ethical ideas and words also makes it easier to communicate with other people around such matters. Finally, being curious about ethics and morality inevitably makes one more aware of one's own moral values, assumptions and biases, and willing to learn.

The following sections explore some perspectives that offer starting-points for assembling one's own pluralist ethics framework: practical justice, relational ethics, Indigenous culture as a moral paradigm, and a human rights approach.

Practical justice

Research ethics training provided for counsellors and psychotherapists, and other psychotherapeutic practitioners, assume that research studies are carried out in a social context characterised by fairness, equality, and respect, or that it can be taken for granted that any structural and institutional injustices that exist are being dealt with by the legal system. Within such an imagined context, the researcher and the participants in a research study can be treated as though they were agents of equal power, status, and access to information. Procedures such as informed consent are designed to ensure that the rights of research participants are safeguarded and to prevent researchers from exploiting or harming them. In short, in conventional research, what ethics committee procedures are trying to achieve is to maintain fairness and justice within the research arena itself, rather than promoting social justice in the wider world.

From a participatory research perspective, contractual ethics protocols are still necessary, as a means of avoiding researcher abuse and manipulation of research subjects/informants, and to maintain public trust. However, such procedures seriously underestimate the prevalence and pervasiveness of injustice and inequality within contemporary society. Far from taking place on an equitable playing field, differences in power and status are played out within relationships between researchers and participants, and most research in fields such as health, social care, and education are exploring problems either have their origins in injustices inflicted on individuals and communities, or have been exacerbated by such factors.

Participatory research can be viewed as a form of practical justice (Aggleton et al., 2019; Patton and Moss, 2019). In a fundamentally unjust world, academic and philosophical analysis can only offer abstract conceptualisations, and the police and the legal system can only deal with specific instances of injustice. This leaves a massive amount of routine oppression that occurs in everyday life, on top of the many layers of intergenerational and historical trauma and betrayal inscribed in people's bodies, minds, and relationships. Aggleton et al. (2019) have suggested that much of the work of social workers, educators, psychotherapists, and others – and the research that supports their efforts – can be regarded as forms of everyday practical justice.

Practical justice involves attention to small ways in which respect, dignity, and worth can be either restored or degraded. An example of practical justice highlighted in the book by Aggleton et al. (2019) is the development and use, in the field of alcohol and addictions therapy, of outcome measures co-designed by practitioners and service users. The chapter by Madden et al. (2019) points out that people who use alcohol and other drugs are widely stigmatised – they are consistently in situations in which other people (including drugs workers and researchers) look down on them and distance themselves from them. Every occasion on which a drug user, in a research study, has the experience of completing a questionnaire that does not reflect the realities of their lives, reinforces that stigma and sense of worthlessness. By contrast, being invited to take part in the development of a more meaningful questionnaire, or filling in a scale that asks appropriate questions, makes a small but significant contribution to a sense of being valued. Over time, the information collected through this kind of user-generated questionnaire is more likely to lead to more effective services, compared to interventions planned and evaluated on the basis of assumptions and beliefs of researchers and practitioners who do not have first-hand knowledge of the experience of living with an addiction.

All of the examples of participatory research on psychotherapeutic topics that were summarised earlier in Chapter 1 can be understood as being driven by a wish to address injustice. In some instances, injustice was at the forefront of the study, such as in the programme of research by Gabriel et al. (2017) into the question of how to support women and their children to move on from their exposure to domestic violence, or the research by Morrow and Smith (1995) with survivors of sexual abuse. In other instances, injustice was implicit, as in the studies of child psychotherapy by Cedar et al. (2022) and Jones et al. (2020) that took great care to position young people as having rights, personal agency, and the capacity for choice.

Relational ethics

Participatory research calls for both the professional researcher and the stakeholder or service user who is a research participant, to be willing to enter an extended and potentially meaningful and impactful relationship with each other. This kind of situation is ethically highly complex, in the sense that a lot of the time it is hard to know what is the 'right' way to be with one another. For example, when a researcher and participant work closely together through the planning stage of a project, they may share personal information and begin to develop a friendship. But is it a real friendship? Both of them may wonder whether it is in the interest of the researcher to be friendly, as a means of motivating the participant to stay in the project. They may wonder what will happen to the friendship once the project ends, or if they bump into each other in a different situation. What does it mean, for other project participants, if the researcher has a special bond with one member of the participant team but not with them?

Other ethical dilemmas may arise around the experience of difference. In other professional situations, there exist many strategies for dealing with differences in age, gender, ethnicity, social class, disability status, and other identity characteristics, such as being formal, and distanced politeness. By contrast, these dimensions of difference are harder to gloss over in the context of mutual involvement in a participatory research study. They may also be relevant to the focus of the study. For example, in a study into mental health difficulties associated with low income, a participant may be curious about the salary being paid to the director of the project. A further relationally challenging aspect of participatory research can occur in the area of trust. A researcher, whose career and livelihood depend on the successful completion of a project, needs to trust research participants to stay involved to the end. This may be difficult for some participants – research studies tend to take longer than initially planned, or require more effort than was originally anticipated. In turn, service user and practitioner participants need to trust that the researcher will report their views and experiences accurately and in good faith.

To some extent, the capacity to weather relational ruptures depends on the emotional intelligence, self-awareness and interpersonal skills of the researcher, and the support they get from mentors and research supervisors. These capabilities require a sufficient degree of ethical maturity (Carroll & Shaw, 2013) – an attribute that is seldom highlighted in the recruitment and training of academic researchers.

In addition to the personal qualities of the researcher, such as being able to be authentic and established connection and trust with research participants, it is also necessary to understand the underlying moral principles on which participatory research relationships are built. Particularly significant, here, are concepts of solidarity and care. As an ethical principle, the concept of solidarity refers to a commitment to work side by side, together, to support each other to combat whatever form of injustice a research study is aiming to address. If a sense of solidarity can be established and maintained, it provides a touchstone that allows relational dilemmas in such areas as intimacy boundaries, trust, and difference to be tolerated. In terms of understanding what solidarity means in practice, it can be helpful to draw on the old idea of a social and moral 'covenant' – making a commitment to pay back what one has received (Brydon-Miller & Hilsen, 2016; Valdez-Martínez & Bedolla, 2020). Another valuable perspective on solidarity can be found in the writings of Jennings (2016), who describes it as an act of publicly signalling one's recognition of the moral standing and worthiness of a person or group (or ecosystem) whose existence, identity, or value is under threat. Jennings (2016) differentiates between three levels of intensity of the expression of solidarity: *standing up for*, *standing up with*, and *standing up as*. Standing up for a person or group involves being an advocate for them. By contrast, standing up with calls for a deeper engagement with the individual or group being supported, in the form of actual personal contact that has the potential to have an impact on one's own sense of self. Finally, the act of standing up as, is an even stronger type of solidarity, based on a willingness openly to acknowledge one's own vulnerability. In the context of, for instance, research into a psychotherapeutic topic such as workplace bullying, a standing up for position might be expressed by arguing for the importance of this topic within the research agenda of the profession. A standing up with position might be reflected through involvement in co-produced participatory research alongside individuals who had been affected by workplace bullying. Standing up would require the researcher to write or talk about their own personal experience of being bullied, or about their own experience of a similar form of adversity, such as microagression.

The concept of an *ethics of care* offers another useful way of thinking about relational ethics (Groot et al., 2022; Lynch et al., 2021). Jennings (2016) suggests that solidarity and care are different sides of a commitment to justice: solidarity is the public-facing aspect, and care is the interpersonal one. Care is a fundamental dimension of being human: all of us have had the experience of being cared for as babies, and throughout life are engaged in a give-and-take interplay between caring for others, and, in turn, being cared for ourselves. Care involves being attentive to the needs of the other, and so calls for a willingness to consistently pay attention to them. Caring also involves giving – sacrificing one's own time, skills, and material resources for the good of the other person. A participatory research team is unlikely to function effectively if they do not care about each other, and care about the topic that is being investigated. Culturally and historically, care-giving is primarily seen as a form of women's work. It is notable that the majority of researchers named in the participatory studies of psychotherapeutic practice listed earlier in this chapter, are women. As with many other areas of women's work, caring is largely unrecognised and taken for granted. For example, care and carelessness are not processes that have been explored to any great extent in the research methodology literature. At the same time, everyone knows what care looks like – listening, empathy, being touched. From a practical justice perspective, the expression and enactment of care – and even love – represent a vital element of ethical practice.

Commitment to solidarity and adopting an ethics of care have the effect of positioning participatory research as a form of mutual aid – people working together to support each other and make the world a better place.

Indigenous culture as a moral paradigm

The cultivation of moral imagination lies at the core of participatory research ethics. The majority of readers of this book are likely to be people who live in societies in which corruption, exploitation, lack of honesty, competitiveness, and lack of care are commonplace, and few positive models of moral integrity are available. All this has the effect of establishing a low baseline for ethical action. Contractual ethical procedures, such as informed consent and confidentiality in research, can be seen as operating to prevent that baseline being breached, rather than functioning to actively promote a positive or hopeful vision of society. At the present time, the most reliable source of a positive moral vision for participatory research is in the ideas and practices associated with Indigenous or traditional cultures. The way of life developed by Aborigine and Torres Straits Islanders, Maori, the first people of North and South America, and other cultural groups in all parts of the world, existed for many thousands of years before it was largely (but not entirely) destroyed by agrarian civilisations and literacy, and then by aggressive and brutal colonial exploitation. Although these cultural groups differed in many ways, there is a broad agreement that they shared a moral framework based on deep respect for the non-human world, a capacity to live in harmony with little violence or war, an absolute commitment to truth-telling and sharing of resources, and an ability to take decisions on a basis of dialogue within the group. A useful summary of this Indigenous worldview is provided by Topa and Narvaez (2022) who present statements from leaders of various Indigenous communities, followed by a commentary on the meaning and implications of those ideas for contemporary life. Roy (2022) characterises the core principles of an Indigenous kinship perspective, for therapy research, as comprising 4 R's: responsibility, respect, relationality, and reciprocity. A valuable account of the implications of an aboriginal worldview for Western science and research can be found in Yunkaporta (2019). There is presently a substantial global interest in retrieving traditional Indigenous knowledge as a means of addressing current issues in fields such as climate crisis, sustainability, and health (overviews of these initiatives: Griffiths et al., 2022; Redvers et al., 2022).

Within the field of research on health, social care, and education, Indigenous academics and other community leaders have mounted a strong and consistent critical resistance to research carried out by outsiders. They have pointed out that mainstream Western research has been not only lacking in respect for their cultural values, but also actively exploitative and oppressive in the sense of generative findings and recommendations that have made their lives worse. A key influence within that resistance movement has been the work of the Maori academic Linda Tuhiwai Smith (2021). Other useful sources are the *Journal of Indigenous Research* and *AlterNative: An International Journal of Indigenous Peoples*.

From a participatory research perspective, the value of the work of Indigenous researchers lies not only in its capacity to critically analyse a dark side of mainstream research carried out from a European intellectual standpoint – shortcomings that are hard for those brought up within that reality to see. It also functions as a source of ideas and methods around how participatory research can be carried out – because that is how knowledge has always been created in such communities. Entry points into this methodological literature include Anae (2019), Hokowhitu et al. (2022), Tuia and Cobb (2021), and Yunkaporta and Moodie (2021). An example of an Indigenous approach to building knowledge that has received a lot of attention is the Aboriginal practice of *yarning* – a structured, respectful mode of talking and learning together in a group that involves deep listening (Hughes & Barlo, 2021; Sharmil et al., 2021).

Unlike contemporary participatory research that needs to work out how to operate through inclusive non-hierarchical relationships, and take account of embodied and non-human ways of knowing, Indigenous methodologies have the advantage of many years of experience around such ways of knowing. Indigenous methodology offers a rich and sophisticated approach to building practical knowledge that places a strong emphasis on the importance of *kinship* (with other people, and also with entities in the more-than-human world) and *place* (the principle that knowledge is inextricably bound to actual places in sites within the physical world). Some collaborations between White and Indigenous researchers identify the place where the study was carried out, in the author list of their academic outputs (Country et al., 2020, 2022; Hernández et al., 2021). A further distinctive ethical theme in Indigenous inquiry has been an emphasis on solidarity. For example, consent for research is not merely an individual decision, but also needs to take account of the collective standpoint of the community (Saunkeah et al., 2021). This represents just one instance of how Indigenous research builds on, while moving beyond, the ethical principles enshrined in the 1979 Belmont Report.

It is essential that oppressive colonialist patterns of appropriation and control are not re-enacted in relationships between White and Indigenous co-researchers. This is a particularly important issue in the context of research into therapy: there exist many examples of misunderstanding, and unattributed use of Indigenous ideas and practices by White therapists around such activities as mindfulness, yoga and shamanism, and in respect of some of the key ideas promoted by Jung (Deloria, 2012) and Maslow (Bear et al., 2022).

An additional layer of ethical sensitivity in relation to the interface between Indigenous and Eurocentric ways of knowing arises from the fact that Indigenous knowledge practices and traditions have been fragmented, and in many instances lost, as a result of colonial violence and genocide, and the assimilation of Indigenous people into Western ways of life. As a result, it has become hard to identify, or draw on, a unified or coherent Indigenous approach to knowledge-building. There have been tensions within Indigenous communities about what counts as Indigenous practice, and what can legitimately be shared with non-Indigenous researchers (Gone, 2017, 2019).

Human rights

An Indigenous perspective on ethical aspects of research invites reflection on the question of whether values, morality, and ethics are culturally specific, or whether it is possible to identify a general set of human rights and obligations. There is clear evidence of the existence of culturally specific values and ethics, not only within Indigenous cultural traditions (e.g., the significance of land and place) but also in differences between individualist and collectivist cultures. For example, in research conducted in individualist cultures such as countries in Europe and North America, it is appropriate to seek informed consent from individual participants. By contrast, in collectivist cultures it is also necessary to find culturally appropriate ways of negotiating consent with the person's family or community, even when individual interviews are being carried out. The 'human capabilities' model, developed by the economist

Amartya Sen (2010), the philosopher Martha Nussbaum (2011), and their colleagues, represents an influential attempt to map out a generic set of human values. The concept of human capabilities refers to what people can do and how they can be, in order to live meaningful and satisfying lives. Various lists of human rights have been developed that cover such areas as the right for shelter and access to food and water, the right to education, security against violent assault, and being in control of decisions about one's own life. Human rights principles (e.g., the rights of the child, or rights of refugees) have been actively promoted by the United Nations, and incorporated into international treaties and legal statute in many countries.

The concept of human rights is highly relevant to counselling, psychotherapy, and allied activities: many clients who make use of therapy are distressed because of violations of their basic human rights. The application of a human rights approach in therapy practice has been discussed by Barbuto et al. (2011), Rasras (2005), and others, and it is a key element of the Multiphase Model of Psychotherapy, Counselling, Human Rights, and Social Justice (Bemak & Chung, 2021; Shillingford et al., 2018). A human rights perspective is implicit in many participatory studies of therapy. Co-researchers may be motivated to participate in a research study because they view it as a means of addressing human rights issues, or because they believe that other studies that have had a bearing on their struggles have not paid sufficient attention to their rights. Some participatory researchers have integrated testimony methodologies, originally devised by human rights activists, into their research with mental health and social care service users (see, for example, Slote et al., 2005). A shared interest in, and commitment to, human rights can function as a means of building solidarity between academic researchers and community organisations.

Ethical guidelines developed by leading figures in participatory research

Within the field of participatory (and related) approaches to research, there has been a wide appreciation of the significance and relevance of an informed and purposeful approach to ethical aspects of this form of inquiry. Leading figures within this tradition have developed ethical principles in relation to this type of work (see Page, 2022, for a brief overview of this literature). Pratt (2019a) summarises the underlying moral rationale for this type of research. Key themes within the participatory research ethics literature include the importance of mutual respect, inclusiveness, commitment to social justice, democratic decision-making, openness to learning, and personal integrity. In particular, the guidelines developed by the Centre for Social Justice and Community Action (2012; see also Banks & Brydon-Miller, 2019) and Faulkner (2004) and the ethics checklist created by Pratt (2019b, 2021b) provide detailed accounts of how these principles translate into action in the context of different phases of a research project, and represent essential reading for anyone considering undertaking this type of work. There exists an extensive and illuminating literature in which participatory researchers reflect on the ethical challenges associated with their work (see, for example, Gabriel et al., 2017, 2018; Groot and Abma, 2020; Loveridge et al., 2024; Phillips et al., 2022; Van Katwyk & Guzik, 2022; Wilson et al., 2018).

Taking ethical responsibility: skills and strategies

Implementing skills and strategies associated with ethical good practice in participatory research can be regarded as a form of *ethics work* that incorporates not only a capacity to design and plan a study in a way that enable it to receive ethical approval but also an ongoing willingness to be aware of situations that call for an ethical response, an ability to recognise the moral hurt that may underpin emotions that may arise during the research process, and associated qualities of moral imagination and leadership.

Ethics work: researcher as moral activist

When ethical issues are recognised as permeating all aspects of research, it can become difficult to know how to describe what practitioners and researchers are meant to *do*. For example, in research, restricting ethics training and the application of ethical principles to issues associated with the process of securing approval from an ethics committee or Institutional Review Board (IRB) to proceed with a study, reduces ethical competence to a set of skills and information that is necessary for the completion of this task. It can be hard to know what a broader perspective on ethics looks like in practice. Does it refer to a general quality of awareness, or capacity to discern moments when ethical decisions need to be taken (Lehr et al., 2013)? Does it refer to as aspect of the personal development of the researcher, such as ethical maturity (Carroll & Shaw, 2013)? The concept of *ethics work* (Banks, 2016) offers a concrete way of thinking about how ethical awareness, discernment, and maturity unfold in the context of being a researcher. Ethics work represents a strand of what a researcher (or any other practitioner) actually does on a day-to-day basis. It is a work activity that sits along other researcher tasks such as meeting with clients and colleagues, time management, maintaining notes and records, and up-dating skills and knowledge.

Banks (2016) suggests that ethics work consists of a set of skills and activities:

- framing: identifying situations that call for ethical clarification, and decision-making; being able to see how historical trauma and oppression are expressed in everyday interactions;
- being an advocate or critic who stands up for ethical principles;
- showing solidarity; reaching out to, and supporting, colleagues and service users who are inspired by similar ethical values;
- curiosity, humility, and willingness to learn, in relation to ethical principles and practices that are meaningful for colleagues and research participants who have had different life experiences or who identify with different cultural traditions;

- emotion work: being caring and compassionate; willingness to accept and explore the strong feelings that arise in response to experiences of injustice;
- reasoning: being able to analyse, makes sense of ethically challenging scenarios and arriving at a practical solutions; being able to explain and justify ethical decisions;
- sensitivity to moral injury, and being able to support people to recover from such episodes;
- consultation and dialogue with others around both promoting what is right, and developing strategies for handling ethically stressful or critical situations; networking with other to share knowledge and experience around ethical issues; facilitating group exploration of moral tensions and choices; and
- discussion and private study around developing a better understanding of ethical issues.

Taken together, these aspects of ethics work call for the development of moral imagination (Jennings, 2016, 2018) in which the researcher has a sense of what might be possible in relation to how groups and communities might function in a caring and respectful manner. They also call for a willingness to resist organisational rules and requirements that deny the humanity and needs of service users, research participants, and employees (Weinberg & Banks, 2019). Some elements of ethics work can be seen as a type of 'moral entrepreneurship' that proposes new moral rules, standards, and procedures (Shdaimah & McGarry, 2018). Perhaps one of the most useful implications of the concept of ethics work proposed by Banks (2016) is that it has the effect of drawing attention to taken-for-granted threads ethically-senstive and moments within the routine tasks and responsibilities fulfilled by researchers, and highlighting their significance in a manner that encourages and enables this aspect of the work to be taken more seriously and developed further. An example of how ethics work can be given more prominence within a team of co-researchers conducting a participatory study can be found in Shimmin et al. (2017) who offer five sets of questions around justice that the group might discuss at different points in the course of their work together. Other examples are provided by Gabriel (2009), who describes the researcher as an 'ethics warrior' who vigilantly scans the researcher-participant interactions for indications that the relationship boundary is being maintained at an appropriate point of balance between over-involvement and under-engaged detachment.

Constructing a research contract

Engaging with contractual and institutional ethical codes, in the form of designing and implementing a researcher-participant contract, represents an essential thread of ethics work.

All research in psychology, counselling, psychotherapy, and other types of psychotherapeutic experience involves interaction with other people and the formation and maintenance of working relationships. Even in studies where there is limited contact with actual research participants, such as situations in which individuals complete online survey questionnaires, the investigator will need to interact with their research supervisor and colleagues, around the design and planning of the study, with those who are able to give authority for data to be collected, and at a later stage with editors, reviewers and others involved in the publication and dissemination process. Where research is based on direct and sustained contact with individuals, for instance, recruiting, screening informants who may be interviewed, and then checking on their well-being after the interview, a deeper level of relationship may be established. There may also be relationships with stakeholders and gatekeepers, such as when the manager or director of a counselling service gives permission for clients to be contacted for research purposes. Contractual research ethics comprises a set of principles and procedures for ensuring that all these different types of researcher-participant relationships are conducted fairly, in a manner that respects the human rights and individual autonomy of each person or group. Other aspects of research ethics pertain to maintaining the reputation and legal responsibilities of the organisation in which the study is being carried out (e.g., university) and not bringing the profession as a whole into disrepute.

These ethical considerations have been developed over many years to deal with the kind of situations that is typical of most research, where the researcher is in control of the research, and the role of research participants, subjects or informants is limited to providing information about themselves (e.g., through a questionnaire or interview), or giving permission to be observed (e.g., allowing their therapy sessions to be recorded). A central focus of ethical procedures in such studies lies in establishing an agreed contract that prevents exploitation and harm to the participant through implementation of a set of procedures that have been approved (and in some cases monitored) by an independent expert body such as an Ethics Committee or Institutional Review Board (IRB).

All researchers undergo some type of initial training in contractual ethics, usually reinforced by periodical refresher seminars and workshops. Practical competence around completing ethics forms usually also requires learning about the specific ethics procedures and priorities that have been developed within the particular institution within which one is working. For example, in response to the research interests of faculty, a specific university ethics boards may have evolved very detailed procedures for approving medical research, or qualitative research, or research in children – or may possess limited experience in these areas. The best way to learn about local procedures and requirements is to talk to colleagues about how a particular ethics board operates in practice.

Negotiating ethical approval to conduct a study involves addressing a set of well-understood issues that have been widely discussed in the relevant literature, regarding such matters as avoidance of harm, informed consent, confidentiality, data protection, risk management, and arrangements for using a secure data depository to make it available for secondary analysis. In addition, ethics protocols need to take account of the needs of vulnerable groups (e.g., children, or research participants who have received a diagnosis of dementia), and specific ethical challenges associated with particular methodologies, such as randomised clinical trials, case studies, physiological measures such as blood samples, qualitative research of sensitive topics, and autoethnographic studies. Engaging with an ethical approval process also requires an understanding of the nature of researcher fraud and procedures for reporting it.

For reasons of space, further information on these standard ethics procedures is not provided here. There are many excellent sources that discuss ethical procedures in counselling and psychotherapy research, including Danchev and Ross (2014), McLeod (2022), Patel (2020), Sieber and Tolich (2013), and Srinath and Bhola (2016). Research ethics guidelines are also available on the websites of most therapy professional associations, such as the British Association for Counselling and Psychotherapy, and British Psychological Society.

Some researchers have reported difficulties in dealing with ethics committees and IRBs, for instance, in relation to not being allowed to speak to potential participants in advance of securing ethical consent – this policy makes it impossible to involved service users or client co-researchers to be involved in the design of a study. Another problem that can occur is that co-researchers may decide that they want to change an aspect of the research that was defined in the approved research protocol. For example, co-researchers may feel that it would be better for a focus group to have a larger number of members, or for items in a photovoice picture exhibition to display the names of participants. Any such changes may involve delay, for instance, if the committee or IRB has a backlog of work and is unable to deal with minor amendments in a timely manner. Or it can place the primary researcher in the position of a go-between who is shuttling back and forward between the committee/IRB and the project advisory group – potentially leading the latter to feel disempowered. A further set of difficulties can may emerge is when participants are able to make choices around how they contribute information (e.g., the choice of a verbal interview or an art-based activity), or may even be encouraged to improvise their own preferred style of generating data. This can lead to a lack of clarity around possible risks, or to a situation where the researcher ends up doing something that is materially different from what was specified in the initial research protocol.

On the whole, citizen and service user co-researchers are unlikely to be familiar with how ethics committees and IRBs operate, and may resent what they regard as unwarranted external interference in a project in which they may have invested considerable time and effort. Researchers who are co-leading participatory studies may feel that members of ethics committees or IRBs do not understand or appreciate what they are trying to achieve, or are too identified with other methodologies to be open to dialogue.

A general strategy for handling issues raised by the ethical approval process is to convene some kind of advisory group from the outset, and to make it clear in the initial proposal that this is an essential element of good practice in relation to the methodology that is being used. This line of argument is strengthened if the proposal refers to existing published studies that have employed a similar approach, and published ethics guidelines and discussion papers, to build a rationale for what is being suggested. Some participatory researchers (e.g., Blakley, 2022) have found that an effective way to handle questions raised by an ethics committee is to invite their advisory group to work through the questions and generate solutions, on a collective basis. It is worth noting that many successful participatory research studies are carried out by well-established research teams, or university-community collaborative networks, that have generated a long track record of undertaking that kind of investigation. Such groups already possess a wide range of experience and credibility around anticipating and managing ethical aspects of participatory research. For a researcher who is planning to undertake a participatory study for the first time, a sensible option, if feasible, is to become a member or affiliate of such a group. Although many valuable participatory studies have been completed outside of established research groups or networks, in such circumstances it may take longer to work through the approval process, and as a consequence it may be useful to factor that possibility into the research planning timeline.

In conclusion, the construction of an ethical contract, in the context of involvement with an oversight body such as an ethics committee or IRB, comprises a key area of ethics work. The researcher or research team are called on to clarify their thinking about all aspects of ethical risk, develop ways of addressing such risks, and explain their approach to ethical risk in formats and language that reach out to different professional and non-professional audiences. All of this is then required to be opened up to independent scrutiny. From a relational ethics perspective, an ethics committee or IRB possess powerful symbolic meaning, evoke strong emotional responses, for both researchers and participants. All cultures, societies, and groups possess some kind of court of judgement in respect of ethical and moral issues. For those doing research, an ethics committee or IRB (or, in some instances, the ethical standards board of a professional association) serves that function. As a consequence, it may evoke images and fantasies around such themes as an avenging or punishing deity, or an all-knowing protective presence. The way that a researcher or research participant responds to such underlying themes, and the emotions that accompany them, will necessarily be influenced by their life experience and personality style. A relational ethics perspective (Gabriel & Casemore, 2009) suggests that ethical issues do not exist in an abstract philosophical space, but are always inextricably bound up with the individual and collective lived experience of those who are grappling with such issues.

Preventing moral distress and harm

A capacity to be on the alert for ethical issues that may undermine a research project through causing distress and harm, represents a further core strand of ethics work.

Within qualitative research, there is a broad consensus that the personal experience of the researcher represents a potentially valuable source of insight. The process of making constructive use of personal experience is often described as researcher *reflexivity*. For example, the previous experience of the researcher, in relation to the topic being investigated, may sensitise them to aspects of the phenomenon that might escape the awareness in other researchers. Some interviews and research participants may be encouraged to talk more openly, if they know that the researcher has undergone life experiences and challenges to their own. However, unexamined personal experience may contribute to researcher bias – a tendency to elicit data, or pay more attention to data, that is consistent with their own personal views and assumptions. Further discussion of the concept of researcher reflexivity, along with suggestions for further reading, can be found in McLeod (2022). Although this dimension of the research process has been most fully elaborated in relation to qualitative research, Levitt et al. (2022) have shown that experienced quantitative and experimental psychology researchers also acknowledge its relevance in the context of their own work.

Researcher reflexivity includes an awareness of moments – for instance during a research interview – when a researcher becomes aware of a potential ethical dilemma. For example, in an interview with a research participant with lifelong mental health problems, on the subject of coping strategies they find helpful, it may become apparent that the interviewee is starting to get upset, because they are finding themselves mentally revisiting highly traumatic events that occurred in their childhood, that they were generally able to keep 'in a box at the back of my mind'. The ethical dilemmas for the researcher, here, are around what to say, whether to continue with the interview, and how to be helpful. Dealing with this kind of *process ethics* comprises a quite different kind of ethical work than that associated with the implementation of ethical consent procedures approved by an ethics committee, because the researcher needs to decide on the spot how to respond, in a situation where there is no straightforward correct or best answer. Useful discussions of this kind of scenario, and how it can be managed, are available in Finlay (2020), Guillemin and Gillam (2004), Guillemin and Heggen (2009) and many other sources.

While ethically significant moments certainly occur in participatory research, because this kind of research tends to involve extended connection between researcher and participants (or between co-researchers), what happens is that the researcher comes to be highly attuned to the future consequences of ethical decisions. Rather than just being an ethically challenging moment at that particular time, being an effective facilitator of participatory inquiry requires a willingness to be continually scanning one's own feelings and awareness around what is happening, to be able to prevent moral distress from derailing the study or having long-term personal impacts. For example, in relation to her case-based narrative studies, Josselson (1996) describes being highly sensitive to potentially harmful future consequences for participants of publishing material that might be misunderstood, or resented, by other people in the participant's life. Etherington (2007, 2009) presents transcripts of conversations with potential co-researchers where she was trying to explore the implications for them, for embarking on a joint study with her.

The type of ethics work outlined by Etherington (2007, 2009) and Josselson (1996) can be understood as attempts to prevent moral distress and harm. In the context of participatory research, moral distress has been characterised by Sunderland et al. (2010) as originating in the researcher's feeling of moral responsibility – there is a moral burden or pressure to do justice to the reality of the life struggles being faced by co-researchers, and to ensure that a research project made a tangible difference. This responsibility is made more acute by being under time pressure, and by the fact that relationship boundaries were often blurred (e.g., a research participant moving beyond the research contract by asking for help with a personal or practical matter). Researchers who had conducted community-based participatory research, interviewed by Sunderland et al. (2010), reported that they expected moral distress to occur, for themselves and their co-researchers. These researchers observed that they had learned how important it was take the initiative to address such moral distress. They also believed that they needed to allow themselves to be vulnerable to these processes and accept that over time they would almost certainly become worn down by it.

Implicit in these efforts is the wish to minimise *moral injury*. The concept of moral injury refers to the effect on individuals of acting in ways that violate their moral beliefs, or observing such actions in others. The initial studies of this process arose from observation of military personnel traumatised by experiences in wars in Vietnam, Afghanistan and Iraq (Litz et al., 2009). It was apparent that such individuals were not merely affected psychologically and emotionally, but also morally. They felt guilt and shame around things they had done, had seen other people doing, or had allowed to be done. Images and memories of these events persisted for considerable periods of time. The person's sense of themselves as a good person, worthwhile or trustworthy person was undermined. Whatever faith the person had possessed (religious or secular) may also have been lost or placed in question. They felt betrayed by those whom they perceived as leaders. Difficulty in talking to others about morally unacceptable events, had negative impacts on family and other relationships. Sleep was affected, leading to further negative effects. Life may be experienced as meaningless, and not worth living. It may be hard, or impossible, to find a way forward into self-forgiveness or redemption. More recently, moral injury has also been used to explain important types of work stress experienced by human service practitioners, such as doctors, nurses, and social workers, for instance, when working in situations in which they are not able to provide adequate care to patients and service users, due to low staffing levels resulting from financial constraints (Morley et al., 2019).

In participatory research, the researcher is not exposed to the same kind of brutal moral violations and tragedies encountered by frontline soldiers, or nurses in COVID-19 wards at the height of the pandemic. The main source of moral distress is the possibility of being responsible for betraying another person who has put their trust in you (Birrell & Freyd, 2006). Betrayal is a distinctive form of moral injury that occurs in relationships where there is an assumption of trust, or trust is important in the context of working together – conditions that are central to the practice of participatory research. While betrayal may occur in other types of research, it is less likely, because relationships are briefer, more boundaried, and more contractual. By contrast, participatory research is a situation that combines high inter-dependency alongside performance pressures, power differences, and multiple opportunities for misunderstanding. In addition, most of those involved in a participatory study are making themselves vulnerable to hurt. Academic researchers are operating outside of their intellectual comfort zone; service user participants are expected to be open about experiences and life events that may be painful to talk about.

Conclusions

Ethical and moral sensitivity and a willingness to stand up for what is right represent core aspects of both therapy and participatory research on therapy topics. This chapter has introduced a range of ways of thinking about ethics, and an overview of some of the activities that might be involved in the process of engaging in ethics work within participatory research projects. The following chapters take these themes further, by exploring how they unfold within different facets of participatory inquiry.

Topics for reflection and discussion

1 What is your own experience of ethical consent (or the experience of someone close to you) in a research study in which you (or they) were a subject or participant? How satisfactory was the procedure that was followed? In terms of conducting a participatory study on some aspect of therapy that interests you, how would you build on your own personal experience: which elements would you adopt, and what would you change (and why)?
2 Reflect on your knowledge and competence around professional ethics, acquired during your training as a therapist, or in other jobs you have had. In relation to what you know about ethical challenges that arise in participatory research or challenges that you anticipate in a participatory study you are planning to undertake, which parts of your existing knowledge are relevant, or could be readily adapted? Which aspects of participatory research might require you to engage in an ethics re-think, or further study or consultation around relevant ethical issues?
3 Read a participatory research study highlighted in the present book that is of particular interest to you. Within that study, what do you imagine might have been the various types of ethics work undertaken by the researcher?

Chapter 3

Aligning with social justice research goals

Introduction

The intensive level of collaboration and participation that is required to produce satisfactory participatory research is only possible when all participants can see that the research topic and potential outputs are both personally and socially meaningful. A distinctive aspect of participatory inquiry is that it is explicitly contextualised within a specific political or social justice agenda to which the study aims to contribute, grounded in an intention to allow previously silenced stories and voices to be heard (Costa et al., 2012). The existence of such an overarching moral purpose motivates individuals and groups to devote time and energy to being involved in a research project and provides a sense of solidarity and shared purpose that allows a research group or network to resolve differences and work together effectively. This chapter looks at various ways that this task has been accomplished in psychotherapeutic research.

Contextualising participatory research

To communicate with professional readers, authors of participatory studies on psychotherapeutic practice topics need to locate their work within debates around current theoretical, professional, and theoretical issues. However, to effectively engage the energies of co-researchers and community groups, they also need to show that their project is oriented towards addressing a specific area of injustice. A crucial aspect of ethics work in this type of research therefore involves building a social justice case that makes the connection between therapy and broader socio-political issues (Chapman & Schwartz, 2012). This is not a skill that is usually emphasised in research training received by psychologists and psychotherapists. The following sections provide examples of how different groups of therapy researchers using participatory approaches have constructed a moral or social justice rationale for their work.

DOI: 10.4324/9781003405818-4

Research with disadvantaged women

The work of Lisa Goodman and colleagues in universities and service agencies in Cambridge, Massachusetts provides an inspiring model of how social justice values, and the promotion of solidarity and practical justice, can inform participatory research in the field of counselling and psychotherapy. The focus of their research programme has been on addressing the mental health, well-being, and life opportunities of women disadvantaged by low income, racism, or other sources of exclusion. The early phase of this initiative was mainly concerned with supporting women who were depressed. This then expanded to consider ways of helping women suffering from domestic or intimate partner violence, and then to the broader issue of trauma-informed care. As well as undertaking participatory research in which women were actively involved and responsible at all phases of a study, this programme also supported the creation and maintenance of practical services (including securing ongoing funding), collaboration across different disciplines/professions (law and psychology), the development of new helper roles, approaches to training students to undertake this type of work, and new model for making sense of psychotherapeutic activities as ways of activating support networks. Research, practice (delivery of services), development of theory, training, and social change were all equally valued and necessary elements in this overall programme. Even when non-participatory research methods were used in some studies, the study is written in such a way that its origins in a broader collective, justice-oriented body of work are made clear. Representative published outputs (that reflect their approach to participatory research) from this group include Baranowski et al. (2017), Goodman et al. (2017), 2018), and Thomas et al. (2018). The wider scope of this programme can be found in the CV and home page of Lisa Goodman on the Boston College website. There are two key pieces of writing that contextualise this work in relation to an underpinning social justice rationale. The first is a book chapter by Goodman et al. (2007) that spells out in great detail the political, economic, and social factors that contribute to depression in women, and the nature of a feminist empowerment approach to resisting these sources of oppression. The other source is a paper by Goodman et al. (2018) that analyses the limitations of mainstream methodologies (such as randomised clinical trials) in respect of their adequacy as means of generating practical knowledge in respect to the real-world adversity and trauma experienced by many women.

The research programme undertaken by Lisa Goodman and her colleagues is probably the most comprehensively realised example of social justice-oriented psychotherapeutic research currently available. Clearly, it is not realistic or possible for everyone using a participatory research approach to aspire to this degree or depth of scholarship, or interconnectedness of theory, research, practice, and social policy. The writings of the Cambridge group acknowledge that they have been fortunate in operating in a city that includes well-funded and liberally inclined universities and charitable foundations, and strong feminist traditions. They also acknowledge that many aspects of their work have been frustrating and a struggle, as well as satisfying. A key implication of their work, for other participatory researchers, is that contextualising research within a social justice or solidarity frame needs to be credible, both in terms of its philosophical and political rationale argued in a detailed and plausible manner, and links with practice being based on what people are really doing on the ground rather than on future hopes and possibilities.

Counselling and psychotherapy for neurodivergent clients

Attitudes towards people with disabilities and the provision of services have represented a major area of social inequality in capitalist societies that have emphasised prioritised economic productivity. In response to these injustices, the disabled rights movement emerged in the 1960s, soon followed by a social model of disability that argued that disability was not primarily a medical issue arising from biological deficits, but was an issue created by an uncaring society. This shift in perspective was accompanied by demands for disabled people to have more of a voice in disability research (Stone & Priestley, 1996).

Within the disabilities field, the area of research into counselling and psychotherapy for neurodivergent clients represents a powerful example of the reframing of the dominant discourse around research and practice. Until quite recently, autism, ADHD, and dyslexia were regarded as life-limiting deficits that could have a major negative impact on individual functioning and capabilities. Sustained campaigning by people diagnosed with such conditions, alongside their families and other community allies, has resulted in a growing acceptance of the concept of neurodiversity as a term to describe the distinctive characteristics of the 10–20% people whose brains function in a different way to the majority of the (neurotypical) population. Important strands within this movement have been the ideas that neurodivergence is associated with particular gifts and capabilities that are not available to those who are neurotypical, and the availability of a wide range of ways that differences in how neurodiverse people communicate and relate to others can be readily accommodated. Within the network of researchers who study the implications of neurodivergence for counselling and psychotherapy, it has been necessary to learn how to engage in relevant ethics work to promote this standpoint. Some of this work has involved re-imagining research methodology, to incorporate a more participatory and co-production approach (Rosqvist et al., 2019; Stark et al., 2021). Other lines of ethics work have focused on providing a rationale for specific data collection approaches that are appropriate and inclusive for neurodivergent research participants (Courcy & Koniou, 2022; Marcotte et al., 2022; Rosqvist et al., 2020, 2023; Williams, 2020), and documenting participant experiences around engaging with such activities (Pellicano et al., 2022). This has been a collective global effort, in which neurodiversity researchers have supported each other to highlight the social justice dimensions of their work (Dwyer et al., 2021).

An example of how these forms of ethics work have opened up possibilities for participant ownership of the research process can be found in a study of what autistic people want from counselling carried out by Hallett and Kerr (2020).

Research with Indigenous communities

An extensive programme of participatory research on counselling, psychotherapy, and mental health services in Indigenous communities in the US and Canada has been in operation for several decades (Gone, 2022). All of this work has referred to a substantial activist movement that has campaigned for Indigenous rights at local, national, and international levels. The outcomes of these initiatives have been to emphasise the significance of traditional community-based and spiritual approaches to emotional healing (Gone & Calf Looking, 2015; Pham et al., 2024; Wendt et al., 2022) and to create a generation of therapists who are skilled in working with Indigenous clients to identify the combination of Western and local therapy activities that they regard as most relevant to their needs (Pomerville et al., 2022). It is not possible to carry out research into therapy and mental health issues in Indigenous communities (or First Nations individuals living in urban settings) in the absence of a partnership with one or more local organisations. Most published studies are explicitly contextualised, within the opening two paragraphs, in an account of mental health consequences of colonisation and historical trauma. Examples of participatory studies that illustrate these principles include Rand et al. (2023), Reeves and Stewart (2017), and Panofsky et al. (2023).

Using critical theory

A significant strand of participatory research aligns with socio-political and social justice perspectives through identification with a "critical" methodological stance (Levitt et al., 2021a,b). The idea that one of the main functions of social science should be to speak truth to power, proposed by Habermas, Marcuse, Adorno, Fromm, and other philosophers in the 1940s, has found contemporary expression in a wide range of areas of critical research and practice around overcoming racism, colonialism, gender inequality, and other types of oppression. These themes are clearly illustrated in the work by Dutta et al. (2022) that uses the idea of *counterstorytelling* to describe an approach that seeks to document the stories, experiences, and resourcefulness of those in society who are powerless and excluded. Although the work of the radical social psychologist Michelle Fine is not explicitly oriented towards mental health and therapy issues, it still carries a great deal of relevance through its focus on social groups such as those in prison, and its capacity to make links between everyday life experience and morally compelling socio-political themes (Fine, 2006, 2013, 2017; Fine & Torre, 2019). These sources also include many detailed descriptions of the kind of long-term personal and relational commitment that is required in effective participatory research. Along similar lines, Charura and Clyburn (2023) discuss the use of critical race theory as a contextual framework for research that is oriented towards social justice outcomes.

Other strategies for aligning with social justice goals

Many other examples can be found of participatory research studies that contextualise psychotherapeutic and mental health provision within broader social and political debates and movements.

In a study by Matheson and Weightman (2021a) where individuals who have received therapy for complex trauma were involved as co-researchers, the rationale for the study as a whole was the aim of privileging the client perspective in relation to debates around this area of therapy practice, and the rationale for using a participatory approach was framed in terms of the personal interests and values of the researcher, and a wish to explore whether participation in research might facilitate client recovery. This was a small-scale project that did not involve ongoing partnership with client support or advocacy groups: the researcher merely recruited a group of service users who were interested in taking part. An important characteristic of limited time-scale participatory research that arises from the energy and effort of a single researcher, or small team of like-minded researchers, such as studies by Matheson and Weightman (2021a, 2021b), Waters et al. (2018), or Wyness (2015), is that they are typically experienced by intrinsically useful and meaningful by all those who take part, regardless of any wider impact. In this kind of valuable grassroots practitioner participatory research, although an intention of addressing social justice issues may be apparent, it is nevertheless largely implicit and understated. By contrast, participatory research that is conducted in partnership with service users, carers or citizen groups, or that builds into ongoing (and sometimes even international) programmes of research, is more likely to need to be explicitly contextualised as contributing to a wider societal or social justice agenda.

A participatory study that explored mental health issues associated with poverty (Thomas et al., 2020) did not merely identify general themes, but instead focused on the impact of specific aspects of UK government policy, such as the stress arising from being required to undergo work capability assessment (Hansford et al., 2019), and its dissemination of the view that people who receive welfare benefits are responsible for the situation in which they find themselves (Thomas et al., 2020). Many studies of health and well-being in transgender individuals have made use of active participation of members of activist organisations and support groups (Katz-Wise et al., 2019; Nieder & Strauss, 2015; Oaks et al., 2019; Smith et al. 2018). Similarly, participatory research into psychotherapeutic processes associated with individuals diagnosed as possessing autism spectrum disorder has been massively influenced by the emergence and growing impact of the neurodiversity movement (Courcy & Koniou, 2022; Marcotte et al., 2022; Pellicano et al., 2022; Rosqvist et al., 2019, 2020, 2023; Stark et al., 2021). The programme of participatory research with young people developed by Pavarini et al. (2019), takes the UN Declaration of the Rights of the Child as its starting point. Further examples exist of participatory studies with justice, inclusion and respect movements in relation to less widely-publicised psychotherapeutic issues such as the experience of living with dementia, an eating disorder, sight loss, and innumerable other topics.

Conclusions

To a large extent, training and research around psychotherapeutic practice are still predominantly conceptualised from an individualist perspective – life difficulties experienced by people are viewed, and researched, at an individual level. Adopting a social justice perspective requires a willingness to 'study-up', by adopting a higher-level frame of reference in which individual problems are seen as arising from institutional and societal forms of control (Chapman & Schwartz, 2012; Harding & Norberg, 2005). This type of 'studying up' is consistent with the increased attention being devoted to the incorporation of a social justice perspective across the entire spectrum of psychotherapeutic practice (Goodman & Gorski, 2014; Winter & Charura, 2023). It is also reflected in discussion around of how different qualitative methodologies can be used to pursue justice-oriented research questions (Johnson and Parry, 2022).

Questions for reflection and discussion

1 Have another look at the opening paragraphs of counselling and psychotherapy research papers that have influenced you (both participatory and non-participatory studies). To what extent, and in what ways, do these studies align with social justice goals and issues? What difference does it make for you, as a reader, if that kind of alignment is present or absent?
2 Reflect on your own research, or a study that you are planning or hope to undertake. How do you view your research as relevant to the struggle to overcome injustice? How would you explain this point of connection to different audiences? How have you introduced a social justice rationale (or would intend to introduce it), in the introduction to a research proposal or in a paper reporting on the findings of a study you have undertaken?

Chapter 4

Nothing about us, without us

Addressing the reality of power and privilege

Introduction

The origins of the slogan "nothing about us, without us" appear to have been within pro-democracy movements in Eastern Europe, dating back many centuries. From the 1990s, this phrase was adopted by disability rights advocates and activists as a means of drawing attention to their demands regarding representation for disabled people in respect of policies that had an impact on their lives. More recently, the principle of "nothing about us, without us" has been embraced by a wide range of marginalised and oppressed groups and communities, and has been expanded to encompass research as well as policy and service provision.

In the field of research in health and social care, and in psychotherapy, most studies have involved researchers analysing and writing "about" clients, patients, or service users. Researchers have been deemed by society as possessing authority, grounded in expertise, to pronounce on the needs of service users, and how to respond to these needs. Alongside political campaigns, legislation, and peer support organisations, participatory research functions can represent a form of resistance to structures of power and control that exist within contemporary society.

Bridging the gap in power, authority, and access to resources that exists between most researchers and most research participants in the field of studies of mental health and psychotherapy presents a substantial challenge for researchers who seek to engage in participatory forms of inquiry. This chapter anchors the discussion of this issue in debates and examples from research into the lives and experiences of members of Indigenous communities. The aim of this approach is to emphasise colonialism as an essential source of unhelpful and oppressive research practice and demonstrate that an appreciation of anti-colonialist strategies functions as a central aspect of carrying out participatory research on psychotherapeutic activities and practices.

The closing sections of this chapter explore how power and privilege are experienced by those who are involved in participatory projects and ways in which these ethical tensions may be addressed.

DOI: 10.4324/9781003405818-5

Underlying roots of power and privilege

The most significant moral and ethical tensions and dilemmas that arise in participatory research are based on deep-rooted structures of power, authority, and privilege. A key aspect of the rationale for participatory inquiry is that it makes constructive use of *differences* between people. For example, in a study of depression, a researcher may possess a lot of knowledge of previous research on that topic, and research methodology, but relatively limited understanding of what it means to be depressed. By contrast, a therapy client or service user involved in a study may have years of personal experience of depression, but little appreciation of approaches to research. The distinctive contribution of participatory research is that it creates a situation in which such differences can be brought together in a way that extends the horizon of understanding of both the researcher and the service user (or other types of co-researchers). Such a scenario describes a meeting between equals, in a situation where differences are fairly readily identifiable and open to awareness.

By contrast, many differences in power and privilege tend to be rooted in historical events whose meanings may be hidden or even denied. Indigenous cultures, such as Aboriginal and Torres Straits Islanders, First Nations peoples in North America, and many other groups, were characterised by a largely egalitarian, often matriarchal way of life in which decisions were made within the community, and power, wealth, and status were not inherited (Ingold, 2005). The destruction of this way of life by European invaders and settlers, from the 15th century onwards, represents a massive crime against humanity whose implications have resonated through later centuries. For example, the slave trade, theft of land from Indigenous communities, and cultural genocide, involved staggering and sustained levels of brutality and cruelty. This whole pattern can be described as colonialism.

In addition to the heartless murder of many millions of Indigenous people, through starvation and being worked to death, colonialism involved dislocation of people from their land or country. Indigenous culture is organised around oral traditions, such as Aboriginal storylines, that refer to specific elements of the more-than-human world occupied by a community – hills, rivers, fish and animals, star formations. By appropriating land for agricultural purposes, settlers fundamentally undermined the laws and way of life such communities.

Alongside these impacts on Indigenous peoples themselves, colonialism also had an effect on the perpetrators of these injustices. Many white people were themselves brutalised through participation in slavery and genocide. European culture developed racist theories, still widely influential, to justify its treatment of Indigenous peoples. The integrity of the Christian faith tradition was compromised by its willingness to collude with, and actively support, the mass murder of Indigenous peoples.

The effects of colonialism, in people living today, are therefore multi-layered and complex. The consequences of these events are still with us, in the form of racism and white privilege. Colonialist ways of thinking about the superiority of certain races are not only overtly promoted by extremist right-wing political groups, but are also internalised in taken-for-granted ways of thinking, feeling and talking displayed by the majority of population. In Britain, we live with tangible reminders of colonialist crimes, in the shape of statues and public buildings commemorating leaders of the empire and funded by the profits of colonial exploitation and murder. Relationships between people of different cultural heritage are distorted not only by racism, but also by while privilege and fragility (DiAngelo, 2019).

As well as colonial oppression of people in far-off countries, the history of modern civilisation includes many examples of exclusion from basic human rights of people closer to home. Until recently, individuals categorised as disabled, having mental health problems, or being gay or lesbian, were locked up and hidden away. Poverty and violence towards women have similarly been denied and hidden.

The common thread across all of these areas is the power of some groups of people to control the lives of those in other groups. Contemporary society is organised on the basis of such structures of power, control, and privilege, which operate within research contexts just as much as they do in other spheres. In mainstream research, such factors are managed by creating a distance between researchers and participants, and limiting the amount of time spent in direct contact. By contrast, participatory research creates a situation in which researchers and participants spend time together, and have opportunities to talk openly with each other. As a consequence, it is more likely that the enduring effects of colonial and other oppressive beliefs and relationships will be apparent.

In response to these factors, many social researchers, and some therapy practitioners and political activists, have sought to *decolonise* research and practice. This principle refers to a wide-ranging set of activities, encompassing attention to the use of language and taking account of Indigenous values, through to initiatives to allow Indigenous communities to regain control of lands that were stolen from them (Tuck & Yang, 2012). In the context of research in the field of psychotherapeutic practice, well-being, and mental health, while a decolonising standpoint is widely viewed as desirable, there is also a broad recognition that it can be hard to accomplish (see, for example, Nadeau et al., 2022).

A key point here is that, in participatory research, issues of power and control are not merely a matter of personality clashes between individuals, or dependent on the degree of self-awareness, interpersonal skills, and emotional intelligence of those who are managing a project. Rather, inequality in status, access to resources and capacity to enforce decisions, are integral aspects of modern culture society. This point is particularly important in relation to participatory research carried out by counsellors and psychotherapists. Historically, most participatory research has been carried out by sociologists, educationalists, social workers, and community development workers who have been highly sensitive to the functioning of structures of social power and control. By contrast, therapy research and training have tended to place less emphasis on power inequalities, and therapy practice has tended to take place in neutral settings (or what therapists assume to be neutral settings) outside of obvious power hierarchies.

Resisting the use of research as a form of social control

Modern science, which emerged at the same time as colonialism, is widely regarded as being objective and value-free, and a benign force for good. These assumptions have been strongly challenged by groups of people whose experience has taught them that, in many instances, research findings have been used to justify and reinforce their marginalisation, exclusion, and exposure to unfair interventions. For example, on the basis of recommendations from educational and social policy researchers, for many years governments in both Australia and North America enacted a policy of taking Indigenous children away from their families and educating them in residential boarding schools. This policy was intended to enable these young people to be better able to enter the job market. In reality, it was enormously destructive of cultural traditions and family life, and contributed to the development of mental health problems and high rates of addiction and suicide. The oppressive use of health research to marginalise Indigenous people is still occurring (see, for example, Goodman et al., 2018).

In response to what they regarded as the use of research to reinforce policies of exclusion and control, Indigenous communities argued that, before colonial times, they had built up a rich and extensive body of knowledge that was grounded in methodologies that were consistent with their own worldview and values, and that what was necessary was to develop an approach to research that combined Western and Indigenous ideas about knowledge. This perspective was articulated in a particularly powerful and influential manner by the Aotearoa New Zealand educational researcher Linda Tuhiwai Smith (Smith, 2021) and the Canadian researcher Shawn Stanley Wilson (2008) who pointed out that Indigenous ways of knowing were based on relationship/kinship with (not control over) both land and people (Topa & Narvaez, 2022). Over the last 20 years, an Indigenous approach to research and inquiry has evolved that draws upon both a distinctive set of concepts and style of thinking (Mehl-Madrona & Pennycook, 2009; Yunkaporta, 2019) and methods for data collection and analysis (Hokowhitu et al., 2022; Tuia & Cobb, 2021; Yunkaporta & Moodie, 2021). Indigenous researchers have also developed strategies for retaining control over data collected by government organisations, such as routine health statistics (Walter, 2010; Walter & Suina, 2019).

Key lessons for participatory researchers, from research on Indigenous communities, are the importance of actively challenging and resisting methods of knowledge creation that serve the interests of the powerful, and developing alternative methodologies that can take their place. This strand of intellectual and academic activity therefore represents a crucial form of ethics work that has the aim of creating inquiry spaces that are (relatively) free from dominant colonial patterns of power and control.

Principles of emancipatory research

Although decolonising and Indigenous research offer the most powerful and sustained examples of how structures of academic power, can be disrupted, it is possible to identify similar processes in other areas of applied research, for instance, in relation to people with disabilities, and survivors of adversity and abuse (including psychiatric abuse). Stone and Priestley (1996) suggested that it is valuable to regard research in such areas as explicitly 'emancipatory' in orientation and proposed a set of guiding principles for studies that embraced such an objective:

1 An underlying theory that emphasised the social origins and maintenance of problems.
2 De-emphasising claims to generating detached, objective knowledge; concentrating instead of practical knowledge that could make a difference to the lives of disabled people and survivors.
3 Only doing research that would be of practical benefit to marginalised people.
4 Reversing the social relations of research production; experts by experience having control over the research process; the research placing their skills and knowledge at the disposal of community members and organisations.
5 Personalising the political/politicising the personal; showing how individual stories illustrated broader collective themes.
6 Willingness to use different methods of data collection and analysis; key methodological criterion was relevance to social justice objectives of a study.

It is of interest that these principles go beyond, in the sense of being more radical than, the approach utilised in most of the participatory therapy studies highlighted in the present book, which is based on involving experts by experience in order to provide additional detail in the context of an investigation that is essentially controlled by an academic researcher. Stone and Priestley (1996) represent a strand of participatory research (a more recent example being the work of Rose, 2018; 2020; Rose & Kalathil, 2019) that argues that professional power and privilege are so dominant and entrenched that full service-user control of research is the only way to bring about real change. Turner and Gillard (2012) reinforce these concerns in their observation that service user voices may have become less influential as participatory and co-produced research has become more mainstream. Further discussion of the struggle of mental health service users to participate meaningfully in research, can be found in Russo and Beresford (2015), and Russo and Sweeney (2016).

Addressing power and privilege within participatory research practice

Within the middle ground of participatory research, where academic researchers and experts by experience operate in partnership, a lot of attention has been devoted to the ethical task of addressing possible ways in which academic/professional power and privilege might lead to marginalisation and exploitation of co-researchers. This issue has been tackled in several ways. First, the concept of epistemic privilege has been used as a means of identifying subtle forms of control. Second, some participatory researchers have conducted research and theory-building around this topic, leading to practical guidelines. Finally, some specific issues have been highlighted as being particularly contentious: money, space, and naming/recognition.

Epistemic privilege and injustice

The concept of epistemic justice refers to situations where someone with authority or status authority (e.g., an academic researcher) acts as though evidence from one person or group is more credible and valuable than information from another person or group. Fricker (2007, 2017) identified two forms of epistemic injustice: *testimonial injustice*, where evidence provided by a person is not taken seriously because of who they are (e.g., a client's evaluation of therapy being disregarded because of their alleged diminished capacity for rationality); and *hermeneutical injustice* when a source of evidence is not well enough understood at an institutional or organisational level for it to be taken into account (e.g., when journal reviewers reject participatory research manuscripts because of lack of knowledge of participatory methodology). The concept of epistemic injustice is a useful way of making sense of what can happen with participatory research teams that include individuals from different cultural or social class backgrounds to the researchers who are leading the project. In such a situation, even if the lower-status members of the group are treated with kindness and consideration, and listened to, what they say is likely to be disregarded. An example of how epistemic injustice can operate in participatory research can be found in a study of crisis care in a psychiatric service, carried out by Groot et al. (2020). In this project, the research team included several service users. When the group as a whole reviewed their work together, at the end of the study, they found that the service user participants reported that their ideas and experiences had been marginalised in a number of small but nevertheless significant ways: they had not been able to contribute fully to the final report because of tight deadlines; one of them had dyslexia and poor writing skills, so was unable to input to the report; and, they had a sense that professional members of the team did not always take them seriously, particularly when they said things that were critical of the service. It is worth noting that these observations emerged from a project facilitated by an experienced and successful group of researchers. Groot et al. (2020) concluded that the cumulative effect of this series of micro-epistemic injustice events had resulted in a gradual disconnection between members of the team. A further aspect of epistemic injustice, not directly observed by Groot et al. (2020) but consistent with their analysis is the phenomenon of "strategic ignorance": a process through which members of privileged groups in society retain epistemic control by "knowing what not to know" (McGoey, 2010, 2019). In effect, what happens is that, when challenged, those with high epistemic status dismiss the arguments of those who have been epistemically excluded, by doubling down – pleading ignorance that anything inappropriate could have taken place.

From its earliest origins and development, participatory research has been motivated by, and organised around, an understanding that epistemic injustice/violence and strategic ignorance are practices that are deeply unhelpful, morally corrosive, and need to be avoided at all costs (Kaulino & Matus, 2021; Novis-Deutsch, 2020). A defining feature of participatory research is the principle of *epistemic inclusiveness*, supported by commitment to creating effective ways to enable dialogue and interpersonal respect. In some instances, this may stretch to *epistemic disobedience*: challenging and subverting dominant ways of knowing.

Research on how to deal with tensions around power and control

Valuable insights into the nature of power relationships and tensions within participatory research teams can be gained from studies that have looked at these processes in the context of ongoing projects. An analysis by Wallerstein et al. (2019) explored power dynamics in an extensive sample of collaborative research partnerships between university researchers and community organisations. All of the participants from these projects, who were interviewed or completed survey questionnaires, acknowledged that addressing power differences represented a major challenge. Their general view was that issues around power and status in research teams tended to mirror similar tensions within the actual communities in which they operated. In terms of constructively working through such difficulties, they identified a number of strategies that they had been able to utilise to good affect: attending closely to oppressive academic language and status hierarchies, the main leader of the project actively and energetically modelling an inclusive approach, allowing sufficient time to address and work through power issues, and prioritising those research outcomes that were most relevant for the community. An overarching strategy involved building from community strengths – identifying skills, areas of knowledge, and accomplishments of non-academic members of the research team.

Pratt (2021a) interviewed individuals who had been involved in participatory research, around what they had learned in relation to effective power-sharing. These informants identified 15 'sites of power': processes and activities that they regarded as important in relation to handling issues around status and control. These included being willing to share personal stories and vulnerabilities, listening to each other and a sense of being heard and accepted, appropriate financial compensation for time devoted to the study, critical mass (a sufficient proportion of people with lived experience or members of the public on the research team), clear ground rules, and being kept informed about the progress of the study. In addition, several informants in this study stated that it was essential to be realistic about the degree of equality that could be attained and to be willing to accept power differences as inevitable.

The preliminary and early stage of a participatory study, when priorities and research goals are being agreed, can be a point where power dynamics are particularly hard to deal with, because academic researchers and community or service user partners have not yet had time to develop a relationship of trust and mutual understanding. Pratt et al. (2021a, 2021b, 2022) carried out research into this issue, including in projects in low-income countries, and identified a number of pitfalls that needed to be negotiated. For example, at this stage in the life of a participatory project, there tended to be tensions around the budget, resources and financial compensation, even when project leaders were transparent in sharing information about these factors. There also needed to be effective and realistic dialogue around potential unintended harms that might result from the project.

The necessity to obtain ethical approval from a university Research Ethics Committee or IRB can function as a source of power conflict at the start of a study (Tauri, 2018). Researchers and non-researcher participants are able to meet and create an environment in which they are able to work through power issues. By contrast, ethics committees may operate as external, anonymous sources of authority, who may reject innovative or culture-specific research strategies agreed by a research team, or demand that additional bureaucratic procedures are introduced.

A study by Denner et al. (2019) explored the experience of academic researchers and other participants who had been involved in a participatory study of enhancing educational opportunities for young people. Their findings particularly highlighted the importance of creating adequate time and opportunities for the group to meet and reflect on its own process. They also found that resolving issues of power and privilege had the effect of changing the focus of the project itself, by raising awareness of the significance of the subtle effects of inequality within the youth provision that was being evaluated.

The findings and recommendations of these studies are broadly in alignment with each other. All of them emphasise the crucial value of reflective group discussion, based on careful listening, as a means of addressing power issues. In addition, they all underscore of understanding that the operation of power, privilege, and control are grounded in the specific culture of the organisation or community within which the study is taking place. Beyond these general conclusions, the studies identify a wide range of different power issues and different resolution strategies that may need to be considered.

Other crunch points: money, space, and recognition

Across the whole participatory research literature, there are three issues that are frequently mentioned in relation to tensions around power relationships: payment, control of physical space, and recognition (whose name goes on the report).

The most common situation in a participatory research study is that somewhere in the team there are one or more individuals receiving research salaries. Other participants may receive lower levels of payment or in some instances no payment at all. This situation is particularly problematic for service user participants who may be unemployed and receiving meagre health or disability benefits. However, it can also be difficult for practitioner co-researchers, who may lose income as a result of research involvement (e.g., as a member of a PRN), or whose manager may need to extend the hours of other colleagues to cover their time away. Even when expert-by-experience co-researchers are paid a salary, it is likely to be at a low level. Masters or Doctoral students running a participatory study may have little or no access to money to pay even minimal travel costs to advisory group members. Unequal access to financial resources can have a number of effects on a project. Some participants may find it hard to attend meetings because of travel costs. It may be difficult to arrange informal get-togethers, such as having lunch or going to the pub, if some group members are on low incomes. Beyond these practical issues, there is also the fact that differences in economic circumstances represent a major inequality fault-line across society as a whole. In effect, one of the key structural causes of marginalisation and exclusion is re-enacted within the project group, in a manner that – most of the time – cannot be fully resolved.

The physical space where a project team meets can evoke issues around power and control. Research who work in universities, hospitals, clinics, and other organisational settings, usually have access to meeting rooms that can be used by a research team. However, for co-researchers who do not have an academic or professional background, such contexts may be experienced as intimidating or may be difficult to reach by public transport. In some instances, entry to buildings, corridors, and rooms may require use of a swipe card, or being checked in by security guards. Ethics work around this area of power dynamics may involve finding and negotiating neutral meeting spaces, or venues on participant home territory.

The question of who is named in research reports and funding bids, and choice of pseudonyms, comprise further sites of power. The order of names (who takes first place) can also be an issue. Some community participants, and even organisations, may wish to remain anonymous, while other may deeply resent it if their contribution is not appropriately publicly acknowledged. An extensive academic literature has been generated around these issues and how to handle them. Entry points into this body of work include Gordon (2019), Guenther, (2009), Heaton (2022), Lahman et al. (2023), and Silverio et al. (2022). Other signs of recognition that may raise similar issues include use of photographs, appearing in a radio or TV documentary, being a presenter at a conference or seminar, or receiving an award.

Inequality and privilege in the world of academic researcher

Some academic researchers may occupy an ambiguous position regarding power and control within a participatory research team. They would typically be fluent and confident in relation to using academic language, exhibit an ability to design and conduct research, and have the status of a university of health and social care organisation behind them. However, at the same time, that same academic researcher may have a precarious employment position, and be subject to research strategy policies that give greater weight to conventional quantitative research designs and randomised clinical trials compared to qualitative or participatory research (Heney & Poleykett, 2022;

Lenette et al., 2019). In addition, the majority of participatory researchers are women, in an academic world in which gender inequality still exist. Also, significant levels of bullying, whether disguised or overt, exist in academic institutions (Hodgins & McNamara, 2019). What all this means is that academic researchers may not always be able to operate from a secure base in relation to providing moral leadership around emotionally-charged tensions around differences in power, control, and privilege within a participatory research team. In some situations, service users and community members of such teams may be in a stronger position in respect of such challenges, through belonging to a supportive peer network.

Conclusions

A crucial aspect of the rationale for participatory, co-produced, and similar research approaches is the intention to carry out research that contributes to practical justice and combatting social injustice. It is therefore highly ethically problematic if patterns of injustice are replicated in relationships within a participatory research team. In many patterns of injustice circumstances, clients, service users are motivated to be involved in participatory research because they hope that doing so will allow their voice to be heard, and make things better for other people in the future. To find, then, that one's ideas and suggestions are disregarded can produce feelings of hurt and betrayal. However, participatory researchers are generally highly committed to empowering non-researcher participants, and the latter often report that the experience of being part of a research project has represented a significant and meaningful step in the direction of recovery. There is therefore a lot at stake, from an ethical perspective. The cumulative learning and experience from those who have been involved in participatory research, suggests that this is an area in which ethical pluralism may be particularly important. There are no simple or standard solutions or procedures for handling power dynamics. Instead, there are many different sites of power, most of them connected to broader social and cultural patterns of inequality and privilege. There are also many strategies that can be used to address these issues. Effective ethics work requires sensitivity to power imbalances at all stages of a project, and a capacity to support a research team to reflect on what is happening and identify appropriate ways forward.

Topics for reflection and discussion

1 To what extent, in what ways, does the legacy of colonialism have an effect on your own life? What kinds of decolonising initiatives have you been involved in, are that you are aware of in within your own community? How successful have they been? If you were planning or carrying out a participatory research study on a mental health or therapy issue, how might you implement a decolonising or emancipatory approach?

2 Over the next two days, pay attention to episodes of epistemic privilege that you come across. This could be in your own life, on in social media, television, and newspapers. Keep a note of these events, in relation to who enacted privilege, who was on the receiving end, and the context within which the event took place (the site of power). What have you learned from this exercise that might be relevant for a participatory research study in which you might be involved?
3 In relation to a participatory therapy study that you might carry out, what would be the ideal setting to hold meetings of the research team or advisory group?

Chapter 5

Building relationships

Ethical aspects of working together to produce practical knowledge

Introduction

Participatory research involves a process of working with a group of people to produce practical knowledge. Such a process requires the development and maintenance of sustained, meaningful, and productive relationships between members of the group (Lauzon-Schnittka et al., 2022). Key aspects of these relationships include the following:

- Interpersonal connection, shared understanding, and common values that provide the motivation to be involved in the study.
- Openness to diversity: capacity to disclose and explore differences in perspective.
- Trust: willingness to talk about what may be painful life experiences (i.e., the topic of the study). Research participants need to feel safe with the researcher; the researcher needs to be able to trust participants to fulfil research tasks and sustain commitment until the end of the study.
- Influence and control: ways of relating that enable shared decision-making rather than one individual or group being in a dominant position.
- A sense of belonging and being included in a group.
- Affection and friendship: being able to handle situations in which some members of the group develop friendships while other do not; individuals becoming the voice or face of the project; dealing with feelings arising from the ending of the project.
- Talking together to resolve problems in relationships or in the group as a whole.

The relational dimension of participatory research can have a major influence on the success of project in terms of whether it achieves its goals. A widely reported characteristic of involvement in participatory research is that it can be relationally messy (Kuriloff et al., 2011), disruptive (MacFarlane & LeMaster, 2022), destabilising (Cook et al., 2019), turbulent (Worsley et al., 2022), and trigger mutual vulnerability (Guishard, 2009). For example, lack of trust may result in service user participants being unwilling to challenge the expert-driven assumptions of professional researchers. Alternatively, fragmentation of group cohesion over the course of a project may

DOI: 10.4324/9781003405818-6

lead to a lack of collective engagement around the final writing-up or dissemination stages of an investigation. The intensity and significance of these dimensions will depend on whether participation is transient and episodic (e.g., stakeholders being consulted on the questions to be in an interview schedule) or encompasses all aspects of a project.

Dealing with relational aspects of participatory research draws on the interpersonal skills, self-awareness, emotional intelligence, and capacity for collaboration of all members of a research group. It usually also requires the ability to facilitate group meetings. These capabilities draw on, and can be informed by, relevant training and theory, for instance, in such areas as group dynamics and teambuilding. However, they also require ethical sensitivity and moral imagination. Most interpersonal ruptures within a participatory research group are associated with an individual or sub-group feeling 'wronged' in some way. There is a lot of scope, over the course of a participatory study, for people to develop a sense of being betrayed and exploited, not listened to, or misunderstood (Worsley et al., 2022). It is also possible that research relationships may reflect and perpetuate unjust relationships in the outside world. For instance, some service user participants may experience university-based researchers as responding to them in ways that are similar to social workers or psychiatrists whom they experienced as patronising and controlling. However, there is also scope for a participatory research group to offer its members an ethically positive and transformative experience in which they felt respected and valued, contributed to something that was socially valuable, and learned a lot at a personal level.

The aim of this chapter is to introduce ways of handling ethical aspects of relationships in participatory research: a key thread within this type of project (Banks, 2016).

Ethics work around maintaining productive relationships

Within traditional, researcher-led studies (both qualitative and quantitative), there has long been a recognition that the relationship between the researcher and informants or subjects makes an important contribution to the willingness of participants to engage with research tasks. For example, Gabriel (2009) suggests that, in qualitative research, the interviewer should seek to develop an 'alliance' with the interviewee, similar to the client-therapist alliance in counselling and psychotherapy (Wampold & Flückiger, 2023). In randomised clinical trial (RCT) studies, data collection is typically carried out by a research assistant or administrator, who over time has the opportunity to form a warm connection with the participant, and represents the human face of the investigation. In participatory research, although relationships between participants and researchers are similar to researcher-participant relationships in other types of study, they are more wide-ranging. For example, there is more of an equal status in respect of shared decision-making and mutual responsibility for outputs, and they spend more time with each other. As a consequence, while relational ethics in conventional research is primarily focused on what happens during fairly well-defined specific events, relational ethical issues in participatory research are more complex.

Relational processes and ethical dilemmas are rarely discussed in detail in most reports arising from participatory research projects, because the primary aim of such studies is to address real-world inequalities, and produce ideas that enhance routine practice. The following sections are therefore based on reflexive accounts where more detailed information of relational processes has been made available. The themes discussed below focus mainly on the question of how ethically sound relationships can be created in participatory research, rather than other ethical dimensions that are also explored by these authors, such as power and social justice.

Caring

In any research study, there is a requirement to engage with colleagues and research participants in a respectful manner, and to relate to each other in good faith, for instance, through honesty, fairness, transparency about roles and responsibilities, and procedures for negotiating consent. These requirements are backed up by monitoring and complaints protocols administered by Research Ethics Committees, IRBs, and professional bodies. In some situations, statutory law may be invoked, for instance, when fraud has been alleged or employment regulations have been breached. All of these formal and explicit ethical safeguards apply just as much to participatory research as in any other type of study – they represent a contract or set of ground-rules that each party enters into, and a point of reference that can be referred to if things go wrong between those involved in a piece of work.

There exists an additional layer of relational ethics in participatory research: the design and underlying rationale of this research necessarily require people to collaborate together who represent different perspectives. In some participatory studies, this collaboration may be relatively short-lived – for instance, an advisory group being consulted on the design of an interview schedule. In other studies, the degree of interpersonal contact may be more long-lasting and intense, stretching across the whole lifespan of a study from initial conception to eventual dissemination of findings. In either scenario, there is an expectation of not only being willing to listen to other people who have a quite different life experience, but also to be able to work together to arrive at a mutually acceptable way forward. To be able to move beyond initial contrasting standpoints, it is necessary to *care* about other members of the research team.

The concept of *care* has been somewhat neglected within the research and practice literature (Lynch et al., 2021; Tronto, 1993, 2013), possibly because it is viewed as a form of women's work that is of little significance in an academic and professional world that is dominated by striving for impact and potency. Attention to the concept of care helps us to be aware of how central this form of moral and ethical commitment is within our lives. We are all interdependent and rely on each other in many ways. Giving and receiving care is therefore massively important in all areas of life. It is particularly relevant in participatory research, because of the requirement for a group of people who initially are mainly strangers to each other, to work together around issues that are typically highly personal and emotionally sensitive (Groot et al., 2019).

A crucial and central aspect of care is *kindness* (Brownlie, 2014; Brownlie & Anderson, 2017). Articles reporting on participatory research include many examples of small acts of kindness in relationships between members of a research team: writing a job reference, giving someone a lift, sharing food, celebrating a birthday. A further aspect of caring is being open to *being moved* (Fiske, 2019) by something done or said by another person. Being moved is a core emotional state that functions to build solidarity and connectedness, by evoking a sense of shared humanity.

Although kindness, care, and affective responsiveness (being moved) are common features of the experience of engaging in participatory research, they have seldom been explored in a systematic manner. A valuable account of how these qualities operate can be found in an analysis of a participatory study that aimed to develop suggestions for how psychiatric services in Germany could become more flexible, innovative, and person-centred (Beeker et al., 2021). This study involved a team of eight researchers (three experts by experience, two senior psychiatrists, two medical students and one social anthropologist). Included within this group were individuals with quite different life experiences and standpoints. Some of them believed that psychiatry was a valuable institution that just needed to be reformed, while others regarded the elimination or drastic reduction of psychiatric interventions to be a social and political priority. What made it possible for these individuals to work effectively together was their willingness to take care of each other. At the start of the project, it was hard to find a suitable location for meetings. Members of the group who had bad memories of medical and psychiatric treatment did not feel safe about meeting in a health centre or clinic building. One member of the group then offered to host the meetings in their own home. The study involved travel to psychiatric centres in other cities, and staying hotels. The expenses reimbursement system in the university required employees to pay for such trips themselves, and then claim back – with long delays in the processing of payments. This procedure was highly problematic for team members on low incomes – in some instances team members on higher salaries dealt with this course of inequality by covering costs themselves. The group also developed a number of strategies for ensuring that those who became emotionally troubled or stressed by the material they were gathering in the study (including the senior psychiatrists leading the project) were supported by other members of the group. The point here is that the process of effectively engaging in a shared process of data collection and analysis was not merely a cognitive task based on application of research skills and methods, but also required involved emotional investment and personal learning on the part of all concerned. These emotional and personal dimensions of the work of the group were made possible by the creation of an ethos of care – members of the group were careful in what they said and how they responded to each other, they took pains to repair any episodes of inadvertent carelessness, and were willing to nurture each other and be nurtured.

Putting in the time

Perhaps the simplest, and single most important, aspect of building ethical and productive relationships in co-produced and participatory research, is to allow sufficient time for trust and shared understanding to be developed, and for differences and ruptures to be resolved (Montgomery et al., 2022). In a programme of participatory research with high-risk marginalised young people in Canadian city, the lead researcher ensured that the project would be embedded within a network of supportive relationships with key community stakeholders (local service managers, practitioners, and researchers) through dialogue meeting with over 200 individuals. The research itself was largely carried out by a group of 21 young people who acted as youth leaders, who joined with the researchers for a three-hour team meeting every two weeks over the course of the study. As well as using that time to plan the research and analyse findings, each session included open dialogue slots in which any member of the team could share their feelings about any aspect of the work (Iwasaki et al., 2014).

In the study described by Beeker et al. (2021), the research team came together on average for a five–eight hours meeting every two weeks over the three-year duration of the study. Each meeting started with an invitation for each participant to offer a brief account of their current mindset, mood, or feelings, and anything that they were struggling with that might call for support from the group. The roles of facilitator and note taker for each session circulated around all members of the group. Robinson (2018) has written about her relationship with co-researchers in a participatory study to determine what support people with Asperger's syndrome felt that they needed. The primary researcher was a neuro-typical person, while the three co-researchers were individual who described themselves as neuro-diverse (i.e., accepting a diagnosis of Asperger's). In this project, the connection that was built up between these co-researchers, over the span of a three-year study, led them to decide to continue to work together for a further five years, on a variety of initiatives that had emerged from their initial work together. Sufficient time may also be needed to allow participants to learn about research and develop the skills necessary for active involvement in a project (see, for example, Harris et al., 2024).

Creating homeplaces

A significant part of the appeal of participatory research is that it has the potential to enable people to come together in a way that offers them an opportunity to share and explore a meaningful and troubling aspect of their personal experience. When sufficient time is allowed for such a process to emerge, being a member of a research team can deepen the individual's insights around that area of their life by hearing other people's stories, and being prompted and supported by others to articulate untold threads within their own story. This kind of mutual engagement can also lead to the production of a powerful and novel shared understanding. This dimension of participatory and collaborative inquiry sits at the heart of the dialogal phenomenological approach to research developed by Steen Halling and his colleagues (Halling, 2005). In one study, a group consisting of mainly trainee therapists carried out a participatory study of therapist experiences of despair in therapy, in which they were all co-participants. They wrote about their own experiences of despair in therapy, read these pieces to each other, elicited further written accounts and carried out interviews with therapists of various degrees of experience, and conducted an open dialogue in their group until they arrived at an agreed set of examples and ideas that they felt able to disseminate through a written article (Beck et al., 2005). Halling (2005) suggests that what happens in such an open-ended group is that a sufficient level of intimacy and companionship is created that participants become more capable of creativity and discovery. As participants become more able to dialogue with each other, they become more able to dialogue with the phenomenon (in this instance therapist despair) in a manner that gets closer to the essence of that topic. In turn, as the appreciation of the phenomenon expands, it creates further opportunities for dialogue within the group. Gupta (2021) suggests that this kind of dialogal phenomenology offers a way of making sense of what socio-political theorists and activists have described as the need for people resisting power and oppression to find safe 'homeplaces' in which they can begin to recover from collective trauma. A similar idea was proposed by Beeker et al. (2021) in their reflections on being involved in a participatory study of psychiatric services in Germany. Towards the end of their project, they realised that they had sufficiently worked through many of the massive differences in life experience and power that existed within their research group, to have arrived at what the cultural philosopher Michel Foucault characterised as a socio-cultural 'other-space' in which people are able to meet as equals.

Friendship

In her participatory study that aimed to explore the ways in which young people might be empowered by working in a youth-run community radio station, Wilkinson (2018) spent a lot of time with her co-researchers, As someone who was about the same age as many of those who were active in the station, and like them a keen user of social media, she began to feel uneasy about the extent to which participants viewed her as a friend, and concerned about the possibility that she might be friendship for running the risk of exploiting friendship for the sake of her own research and career interests. She dealt with this dilemma by providing participants with clear information about her research role and its temporary natures, and routinely checking out with them whether they were comfortable about her using what they were saying to her for the research: "are you telling me this as a researcher or as a friend?" However, she described herself as remaining troubled by this ambiguity throughout the study.

The process of forming collaborative relationships in participatory research inevitably raises ethical issues around role boundaries. As well as becoming friends with co-researchers (or resisting their wish to become friends), some participatory researchers use friends and family members with relevant experiential knowledge as consultants and advisors to their studies, or use their friendship network to meet other people who might fulfil such roles or to introduce them to potential interviewees. Tillmann-Healy (2003) suggests that many qualitative researchers use friends and family in these ways without explicitly acknowledging this practice in their dissertations or published articles, and offers a valuable perspective around how to navigate one's way through the ethical issues associated with this way of working. A further useful source on making sense of mixed personal-professional relationships in qualitative and participatory research is provided by Lieblich (2006) in her discussion of being a well-known public intellectual doing participatory life story research in Israel – a small country in which there are many potential points of connection between individuals.

Different types of personal relationship issues can emerge in participatory research with therapy practitioners. Youn et al. (2019) describe the difficulties involved in co-ordinating and holding together inputs from a large number of therapists involved in a multi-university student counselling/psychotherapy practice research network in the US. What turned out to be crucial to the success of this endeavour was the intentional use of local champions who operated as go-betweens between the researchers and therapists engaged in the study, on the basis of the strength of their personal relationships with members of each group.

As with other aspects of relational ethics, it is not possible to formulate predetermined guidelines around how best to handle the issue of friendship in participatory research. What seems to be important is to be willing to reflect on the implications of the types of relationship intensities that are developing, and then being willing to engage in sufficient open dialogue to reach a point of resolution.

A notable aspect of the field of participatory research as a whole is the existence of long-lasting collaborative projects that are built on enduring friendship and mutual loyalty between individuals employed in different organisations.

Facilitating group cohesiveness

Alongside relationships between individual members of a participatory research team, there also exists a collective, group-level relational network. It is difficult for person-to-person relationships to be productive if the research group as a whole lacks cohesiveness, is riven by conflict, or exhibits a toxic group culture. A large-scale study of group functioning in participatory research team found that differences in skill-set and life experience between members tended to be experienced as valuable because they opened up different perspectives and sources of knowledge (Chandanabhumma et al., 2023). However, differences in race, gender, and educational background were more likely to be seen as sources of tension that needed to be worked through.

An important strand of ethics work is to ensure that the research group or team operates in a way that allows each member to feel included, have a sense of being able to influence control over what is happening, and to give and receive affection. Participatory research teams accomplish these tasks in many different ways, such as spending time together, holding open meetings to reflect on the process of the group, making use of external independent facilitators and consultants, or having fun together. A consortium of community participatory research organisations published a handbook of 'promising practices' that they had found valuable in developing and maintaining group functioning (Engage for Equity Research Team, 2017). These activities include worksheets and exercises on such topics as dialogue, listening, conflict management, leadership, participatory decision-making, trust, and reflexivity. They have also carried out research into the acceptability, relevance, and helpfulness of specific group activities (Parker et al., 2020; Sanchez-Youngman & Wallerstein, 2018). An example of an activity that many research groups found particularly helpful was the "partnership river of life", in which all members of a group worked together to use a river metaphor to co-create a historical timeline of their collaborative journey. As well as allowing individual members of the group to deepen their interpersonal bond or connection by interacting with each other in a playful yet meaningful and serious manner, this exercise made it possible to build group cohesion on the basis of shared stories, mutual understanding, and sense of common purpose. The river metaphor was readily adaptable to local circumstances by using bridges, dams, or rapids to express barriers, and tributaries to indicate points where new members or organisations joined the project. Participatory researchers in the field of counselling and psychotherapy, who have a background in group therapy, are able to draw on a rich array of group process models and activities that can be adapted for use in a research context (see, for example, Ogrodniczuk et al., 2021).

Conclusions

Participatory research is fundamentally relational, in the sense of using the human capacity for dialogue and collaboration as a basis for generating practical knowledge. Involvement in participatory research is not only a cognitive/intellectual and ethical experience – it is also an intensely relational one. The relevance of a relational approach to pluralistic ethics is highlighted across all chapters in the present book. All individuals involved in a participatory study bring their own relational competencies and strengths as well as their areas of relational vulnerability and awkwardness. Effective participatory research requires paying constant attention to relational processes and willingness to benefit from relational lessons learned in other studies.

Topics for reflection and discussion

1 Read the study by Groot et al. (2019) on the experience of mutual care in members of a participatory research project. This article is published in an open access journal and is therefore readily available. It provides a unique insight into the points of caring connection between members of a research team investigating psychiatric care. As you read, make a note of phrases or passages that particularly resonated

with you. What is the significance of these moments for your own involvement in participatory research?

2 What are the pros and cons of friendship as a basis for co-researcher relationships?
3 In what ways might an understanding of relationship dynamics in Indigenous communities be relevant in participatory research in therapy?
4 How can participatory research in therapy accommodate the ideas and contributions of individuals (both academic researchers and client/service user co-researchers) who do not function well in relational spaces, and might be unwilling to be involved in a participatory project?
5 Imagine a participatory study of therapy that would wish to carry out yourself. Take a few minutes to make notes of what this study might entail, in terms of who might be involved, and how data might be collected and analysed. Looking at your outline research plan as a whole, what might be some of the potential relationship tensions and conflicts that might occur? As the leader, or one of the leaders, of the project, how might you handle these tensions and conflicts? How might the project be structured and organised, in order to anticipate and prevent or mitigate these difficulties? If you see the difference and tension between individuals as potential sources of growth and learning, how might these processes be constructively facilitated? What kind of training, support, supervision, or external consultation might be helpful for you in being able to fulfil these relationship-building (and repairing) tasks?
6 In what ways might therapy theories around relationships (e.g., attachment, countertransference, family systems, Rogers' model of acceptance, empathy and congruence) be relevant to and understanding of relationships between members of participatory research teams? In what ways might it be helpful (or unhelpful) to draw on therapeutic ways of being/relating when facilitating a participatory research group?
7 The therapy ethics literature, and therapy training, have tended to place a strong emphasis on maintaining clear relational boundaries between clients and therapists. To what extent, and what ways, are therapy boundary concepts and practices relevant in participatory research contexts? In respect of areas in which they lack relevance, or may even be counter-productive, how might relationship boundaries be negotiated?

Chapter 6

Beyond averages

Respecting uniqueness and diversity

Introduction

Historically, within the field of research in counselling, psychotherapy, well-being, mental health, and cognate areas of practice, data collection and analysis have proceeded on the basis of aggregating data from multiple participants. Although this approach is most clearly apparent in quantitative research, it is also exhibited in qualitative studies that report findings in terms of themes or categories that are intended to represent the general experience of participants across the whole of the sample of people included in the study. Research findings based on averages (or on the use of similar concepts such as 'general', 'typical', 'median', or 'modal') are ethically problematic because they do not do justice to the uniqueness and diversity of both individual experience and the experience of groups of people who are marginalised or excluded. This chapter offers an overview of these issues in the context of participatory research. The first part of the chapter considers the logical and societal implications arising for the use of averages in research. The focus then turns to the challenges faced by participatory research teams around addressing issues of exclusion and marginalisation. The closing section explores alternative ways of analysing and reporting data.

The problem with averages

The idea that there exist 'average' patterns of behaviour makes a lot of intuitive sense, and has provided the bedrock for almost all studies of therapy processes and interventions. For example, several hundred studies have evaluated the effectiveness of therapy in terms of a reduction in the average number of symptoms (or average ratings of symptom severity) between the start of therapy and when it finishes. Everyone understands that average change conceals differences – there will always be some clients whose reported change is greater, or less than the average. Nevertheless, most people are happy enough to accept that there will always be a few outlier cases who tend to cancel each other out within a large enough sample, and that average change scores provide a sufficiently accurate picture for most practical purposes.

DOI: 10.4324/9781003405818-7

However, statements that are derived from a *group* level of analysis do not necessarily hold at an *individual* level. Many compelling examples of this discrepancy have been collected by Todd Rose, a psychologist and educational researcher at Harvard University (Rose, 2016). For instance, in the period following the Second World War, the US airforce experienced an alarming increase in plane crashes and pilot fatalities. Careful analysis of each incident suggested that these events could be mainly attributed to pilot error rather than problems in maintenance. Attention was focused on cockpit design, on the assumption that military aircraft had become technically much more sophisticated, with the consequence that pilots had to deal with more information. Aircraft designers also wondered whether the average height of pilots had increased since the standard cockpit layout was introduced in the 1920s. A huge effort was then undertaken to measure the average dimensions of pilots, for example in terms of height and reach, and to re-design cockpits in line with these metrics. However, this did not have any impact on number of accidents. One of the technical staff involved in this project then took it on himself to re-analyse the pilot data in terms of the proportion who corresponded to the average, or were within 10% of the average. He found that only a very small percentage met this criterion – the majority exhibited a wide range of patterns of non-averageness. The decision was then made to accommodate this diversity by making cockpit controls and seating adjustable. This immediately resulted in a dramatic reduction in accidents.

The implication of Rose's (2016) story of how the US air force reduced fatal accidents is that analysing data in terms of averages can conceal important patterns that may be highly relevant for practice.

At the present time, health policy and practice are almost entirely informed by research evidence based on averages. An increasing number of both healthcare practitioners, and philosophers interested in the logic of scientific research, have argued that such an approach fundamentally misunderstands the nature of causality. At the heart of their argument is the suggestion that a causal explanation such as '12 sessions of CBT results in a reduction in depression symptoms' does not adequately reflect the way that causality operates in the real world. They propose, instead, that being offered CBT, or being offered specific CBT activities by a therapist, functions to 'afford' a range of possibilities to the client. Some clients may be disposed to embrace CBT and actively use it to transform their lives. Others may be disposed to engage in some aspects of therapy but not others, while yet others may be disposed to reject it entirely because it is not compatible with their personal or cultural beliefs and values. So, although an overall average improvement may be observed by a researcher who adds up all the change scores, this conclusion is not in fact very useful for a therapist (or for a prospective client). The therapist, for example, is likely to be more interested in which sub-group a particular client falls into. A useful source in relation to these ideas can be found in Anjum et al. (2020), and an associated website https://causehealthblog.org. An account of the relevance of this critical perspective for research and practice in psychotherapy has been produced by Oddli et al. (2023).

A further difficulty with the concept of averages is that it can be interpreted as implying that 'average' means 'normal' and that 'normal is good'. This line of reasoning would be disputed by most researchers, who would argue – correctly – that averages and means are neutral technical concepts within statistics and have no broader moral significance. However, the link between averages and normality is reinforced by use of the term 'norms' in relation to interpreting assessment scores on personality or symptom measures. The pursuit of normality and pressure to be normal represent powerful aspects of contemporary cultural life (Creadick, 2010; Sysling, 2021). There are many people who seek therapy because they have felt crushed by such pressures, and who have experienced a willingness or freedom to be different as crucial aspects of their journey towards recovery. Rose (2016) provides many vivid examples of being exposed to such experiences, including in respect of their own life. Even within mainstream psychology and social science, there are many academics, not particularly identified with participatory and social justice research, who believe that, to become more practically relevant, research needs to be much more attuned to heterogeneity (Bryan et al., 2021).

Representativeness in participatory research

In studies where the researcher conducts an investigation *on* a sample of people, each informant or research subject can be classified in terms of identity markers such as age, gender, social class, illness experience, and other variables. By contrast, in participatory research *with* service users or members of the public, it is not straightforward to determine the representativeness of each member of the research team. This is because the individual is not merely providing slices of information, but is engaged as a whole person who may bring many different aspects of self to the research process. In addition, in a participatory study, an individual who is operating as a service user co-researcher is not merely there to respond on the basis of their own personal experience, but is also expected to be able to draw on their knowledge of other patients and carers they have encountered.

In many studies, only one (or a small number) of service user participants are recruited. Vojtila et al. (2021) described a study of therapy for psychosis, in which one service user was involved. Although this individual, who had undergone a psychotic episode in her own life, made a valuable contribution to the study, she could not in any sense be regarded as representative of the wide range of people who become psychotic. For example, she was someone who had received different types of therapy, and had the confidence and motivation to be an advocate for patients' rights – attributes that allowed her to be an active and resourceful member of the team, but at the same time were qualities that would not have been shared with other former patients.

Locock et al. (2017) interviewed 38 people who had been involved in health research, as patients, carers, or members of the public, around what they brought to their participation. One of the key questions they were interested in was the extent to which these individuals could be viewed as representative of patients, carers, or concerned citizens as a whole. The majority of those interviewed by Locock et al. (2017)

had been invited to join participatory research teams because of their experience as patients with a specific medical condition. However, they reported that, once inside the research team, they fulfilled different functions. They conveyed a sense of what it was like to be seriously ill, including breaking down in meetings as they described harrowing moments. They also supplied specific technical illness information around what it was like to experience certain symptoms, take particular types of medication, or find their way around the healthcare system. Finally, they were aware of fulfilling the function of being a challenging insider within the research team, for example, through questioning the theories and assumptions of the academic researchers. They talked about how they shifted from one role or identity to another over the course of a study, and how their way of fulfilling any of these roles changed as they gradually became more assimilated into a medical research culture. Varied service user research roles were also identified in a similar study by Maguire and Britten (2017, 2018). Further themes that emerged in the Maguire and Britten (2017) were the somewhat arbitrary process used to select expert-by-experience co-researchers, and the observation that some of the individuals they interviewed tried to enhance the representativeness of their inputs to the research in which they were involved, by referring back to service user organisations to which they belonged. The analysis of the same interview data in Maguire and Britten (2018) highlighted some of the tensions that arose for research consultants, such as resisting attempts to tokenise their involvement, while also documenting the experiences of participants who had been involved in multiple projects in different universities over several years. Reynolds and Beresford (2020) used in-depth interviews to depict the trajectories into and through being a service user co-researcher, of five individuals with extensive experience in such roles. An important emergent theme in their analysis was the meaning of research involvement as a career and way of making a living.

Vat et al. (2017) provide a context for these findings by outlining the different strategies used by research organisations to recruit service user research participants, including individual contact, liaising with clinics and service user groups, through to open advertising using social media. Each strategy produces a different type of representativeness.

Strategies for respecting uniqueness and diversity in participatory research

Sensitivity to diversity is a crucial aspect of participatory research – social justice, care, and solidarity are all undermined when the experiences, stories, and insights of individuals or sub-groups are missing in the results of a study. Strategies for addressing this issue include analysis in terms of trajectories and cases, research team members as representatives of specific communities and organisations, a programmatic research perspective, and using the concept of intersectionality.

Analysis in terms of trajectories and cases. Most therapy studies – whether qualitative or quantitative – report findings in terms of averages, central tendencies, or general patterns. Alternative or supplementary ways of analysing and presenting findings can be based on trajectories and presenting cases. For example, in the field of research into therapy and emotional difficulties in young people, some researchers have not aggregated themes and scores across their entire sample, but have looked for patterns or trajectories (e.g., pathways through therapy) of specific sub-groups (see, for example, Arizaga et al., 2020; Gibson & Cartwright, 2014; Stige et al., 2021). Other researchers – including in several studies highlighted in the present book – have chosen to present such patterns as case examples.

Research team members as representative of specific communities and organisations. In participatory research, non-academic co-researcher members of a research team can be recruited on the basis that they belong to a wider community, and would be able to refer back to that community to access a broader perspective on the topic that includes but is not restricted to their own personal experience. This approach is widely used in participatory research that is carried out in partnership with community organisations and Indigenous tribes/communities.

A programmatic research perspective. In situations in which it is possible to sustain an ongoing programme of research, it is possible to acknowledge limited representativeness in one study and then use a subsequent study to fill that gap. Alternatively, the unique story of an individual, that cannot be accommodated within a study report for reasons of space or coherence, could then be the subject of a further stand-alone paper.

Using the concept of intersectionality. The concept of intersectionality refers to the fact that commonly used social and demographic identity markers, such as age, gender, social class, race, sexual orientation, and disability status, are limited in respect of the extent to which they can usefully inform policy and practice in social and health care, and in psychotherapy (Bryant-Davis, 2019; Moradi & Grzanka, 2017). This is because, for example, the experience of being an adolescent is not the same for all people aged 14–18. The experience of being an adolescent is quite different for a White, male, middle-class, heterosexual, 16-year old, compared to someone of the same age who identifies as a Black, female, lesbian, refugee. The concept of intersectionality is extremely difficult to incorporate into research that is based on averages and representative samples, because it is rarely feasible to devise ways of accommodating the level of identity complexity that might be involved. By contrast, intersectionality can be seen as a potential gift for participatory research, because community members of a participatory research team are likely to have clear ideas about the particular identity intersections that are most relevant to their own experience of the topic being investigated. In addition, adopting an intersectionality perspective provides strong intellectual rationale for focusing in the multiple identity patterns that emerge as significant within a particular study, rather than trying to justify results in terms of broad-brush socio-demographic categories.

Although these ways of accomplishing a greater capacity for reflecting diversity and uniqueness in a participatory study are under-used in the research literature, they are out there, and it is not difficult to find exemplar studies that utilise them, that can serve as models for one's own research.

Conclusions

Ensuring that uniqueness and diversity are respected represents an important strand of ethics work in any participatory research project. If the views, voices and experiences of sub-groups of people, or individuals, are not allowed expression in a study, it is hard to claim that the investigation is making a genuine commitment to overcoming injustice. Exclusion of potentially relevant perspectives and observations is likely to reduce the practical utility of research findings. For co-researchers, a sense that their own inputs are being disregarded in an effort to attain a consensus or general findings may be felt as a betrayal. However, despite these important ethical issues, most participatory research studies continue to report findings in terms of average themes or patterns, and devote limited attention to the extent to which service user co-researchers are representative of the domain of client or patient experiences as a whole.

Topics for reflection and discussion

1 Read any therapy research paper that is interesting and relevant for you, that analyses data in terms of general themes or average scores. Imagine the group of people who have contributed data to this study – how diverse were they? Information about the research sample should provide you with clues to the range of different experiences that were encompassed in the study. In relation to the findings of the study – whose life experiences are being ignored or downplayed? To what extent, and in what ways, could greater attention to these silenced or redacted voices enhance the meaningfulness and practical value of the study?
2 Read the study by Reynolds and Beresford (2020) on the experiences of people who have been involved in participatory research. This study is published as an open-access article and is readily available. It also discusses issues, around the meaning of participatory research, that are central within the present book. Reynolds and Beresford (2020) present their findings in terms of five carefully described case studies. Having read their work, how do you see the advantages and disadvantages of case-based analysis as opposed to an average-based approach?
3 Identify a participatory study that you would like to undertake, into some aspect of counselling, psychotherapy, or recovery. How many service user, client, or community co-researchers would you aim to include in your research team? How might you go about ensuring that these individuals were sufficiently able to represent the broader client or service user, not just statistically (e.g., age, gender) but also in respect of the particular aims and focus of the study?

Chapter 7

Responding ethically to the personal challenges and opportunities associated with research participation

Introduction

Morality and ethics represent what is possibly the most basic level at which a person relates to other people and to the more than human world. Academic research based on the collection and analysis of quantitative data is primarily a cognitive and rational activity that generally does not require the researcher to reflect deeply on their assumptions about who they are, what is right or wrong, or what is real. By contrast, in requiring the researcher to be open to the experiences and worldview of others, qualitative and participatory research opens up the possibility that research process will produce moments at which the researcher find that their beliefs and values – and even their core assumptions about reality (ontology) and what counts as knowledge (epistemology) – are questioned and challenged. Such events – at least at the time when they are happening – are unlikely to be experienced in ways that allow for ready categorisation or interpretation. Instead, they may be expressed in the form of vague feelings of discomfort, uncertainty, dread, confusion, anxiety, and guilt. There can be a sense that the research process possesses a personal significance that demands to be grasped. At the same time, being a member of a participatory research group can also be supportive, fun, and personally satisfying. The present chapter offers an overview of some of the main personal challenges and satisfactions associated with involvement in participatory research and also considers the implications of these processes for research training and practice.

The personal meaning of involvement in participatory research

Participatory research takes many forms and can be carried out at different levels of intensity and over different time-periods. The topics being addressed in participatory research also vary in relation to their cultural and personal sensitivity. Different members of a project group may be affected in different ways.

The personal meaning and impact of involvement in participatory research is similar to, and overlaps with, the experience of engaging in qualitative research. There

DOI: 10.4324/9781003405818-8

exists an extensive literature around the ways that both researchers and participants are affected by the qualitative research process. On the whole, participants interviewed in qualitative studies tend to describe their experience as having been interesting, stimulating, and personally valuable (Lakeman et al., 2013). Those conducting qualitative research describe a range of reactions. There can be a sense of intense moral responsibility in respect of being privileged to hear people talk about painful and private life experiences (Oakley et al., 2022). This can be accompanied by moral distress (Sunderland et al., 2010) and guilt (Josselson, 1996) around the possibility of letting informants down or not living up to one's own moral standards. Qualitative researchers report a mix of emotional responses during and after interviews, including a sense of being moved by what an informant has said, painful personal experiences being triggered, fear-inducing intrusive traumatic images, and feelings of closeness and affection (Granek, 2017). It is not unusual for qualitative researchers to encounter moments of deep moral and ethical uncertainty during an interview, when they feel they may be on the verge of pushing an informant too far, or opening up areas of informant deep personal hurt or shame (Guillemin & Gillam, 2004; Guillemin & Heggen, 2009). The cumulative effect of all of these processes can be exhaustion – an experience of being immersed to overflowing in the stories one is hearing (Doucet, 2008).

Key elements of the experience of involvement in participatory research

While it is not helpful to think in terms of any kind of general model of how people are touched or changed by their involvement in participatory research, it is nevertheless possible to identify some general processes that are characteristic of participatory research studies that can make this kind of activity particularly powerful at a personal level: time, narrative, dialogue, and emotion.

Time

A distinctive aspect of participatory research is the amount of *time* that the researcher and participant/informant spend with each other, and the quality of that time in respect to the type of interaction that takes place. In quantitative research, for example, where a research participant completes a questionnaire, the contact between a researcher and a research subject may be quite brief. Even when there are longer or regular meetings (e.g., a researcher sits with a client at the end of each session while the client completes a batch of forms) the interaction is mainly limited to practical issues around such matters as how to interpret instructions on a questionnaire, or whether it is necessary to answer all items. In qualitative interview-based research, the researcher interviewee may be in contact for a brief pre-interview screening or assessment conversation, and then for perhaps a single interview lasting one to two hours, and then possibly also for a follow-up to check the informant's well-being or to check whether they are satisfied with the accuracy of the interview transcript or the researcher's analysis of themes in the transcript.

In contrast to these other types of research, participatory studies involve much more contact time, typically spread out over an extended period. Participatory research is similar in some respects to fieldwork-based qualitative ethnographic or participant observation research in which the researcher and participant may spend a lot of time together in a variety of situations. The amount of interpersonal contact associated with participatory research makes it possible for trust to be developed, and for the researcher to have more than one opportunity to explore sensitive topics. It also provides space in which misunderstandings and relationship ruptures can be repaired. However, ending the research relationship may be more problematic. Whereas in most quantitative and qualitative studies there is a clear mutual understanding from the start regarding how many meetings there will be, and when the contact will case, participatory research depends on a collaborative relationship whose end-point is hard to predict.

Narrative

As in qualitative research that uses one-off interviews, participatory research usually involves participants telling their story of what happened in relation to the topic or issue being investigated. This *narrative* focus can have powerful effects on both researcher and non-researcher participants. While the experience of telling one's story can be emotionally freeing and liberating, it can also be disturbing and troubling to remember painful events, and there may also be a sense of shame, embarrassment, or vulnerability around sharing private information with another person. For the researcher listening to, and recording, the story, the experience may involve a sense of closeness, compassion, and solidarity, a feeling of being responsible for doing justice to the informant's life, and also in some instances a reaction of being shocked, afraid, angry, and even traumatised at the images and events that one is learning about.

Dialogue

A defining characteristic of participatory research is that it involves people with different perspectives coming together and sharing their experiences and knowledge in dialogue with each other. There is a broad consensus that the process of engaging in open, democratic, or authentic dialogue has the potential to generate new insights and practical knowledge, through allowing individuals to learn from each other and build bridges between contrasting ways of seeing an issue (Seikkula & Trimble, 2005; Stewart & Zediker, 2000). A lot of the time, people communicate through monologues in which they engage in a one-way process of communicating information, or their opinions, to the other person (or group). In other situations, people may interact with each other in the form of an argument – responses to the other are mainly intended to reinforce one's own position and convince the other person that they are wrong. By contrast, dialogue involves listening to what the other person has to say, and working together to find points of connection. Stewart and Zediker (2000) describe the essence of dialogue as *letting the other happen to me* while at the same time *standing my own ground*. When this happens, the person becomes able to move beyond their pre-existing ideas, and learn something new. When this combination of listening, while also being willing to share one's own views, occurs in a group, it creates the possibility for establishing a community of inquiry (Sharp, 1987) in which several people learn at the same time.

Emotion

The process of participatory research can be experienced with the expression of strong emotions. Most participatory research focuses on topics associated with adversity, injustice and suffering – members of a research team with lived experience of the issue being investigated may carry strong feelings about what has happened to them in their lives, and may tell stories about their experience that convey these emotions to other members of the team. There can be passionate beliefs about how the research should proceed, and how to ensure that it is carried out as well as it could be. Relationships between members of a research team can evoke feelings that originate in earlier relationships in a member's life – one of the university researchers may wear their ID badge on a lanyard around their neck, similar to the lanyard worn by the social worker who took that individual into care. Over the duration of a project, members of the team may experience emotionally charged life events – marriages, divorces, bereavements – that they bring into meetings.

Any of these elements of the research process – time, narrative, dialogue, emotion – can have a personal impact on a member of a participatory research team. All of them represent sites of ethics work, for example, in terms of ensuring that they occur within a context or care and that individuals are not silenced or excluded, or emerge with a sense of having been tokenised, betrayed or morally damaged. A further aspect of ethics work around these themes is concerned with positive moral leadership, expressed through actions that are affirming of team members, and celebrate individual and collective accomplishments.

What people say about their involvement in participatory research

Although several participatory research groups have written about 'lessons learned' from specific projects, there have been relatively few published accounts of the personal meaning, experience and impact of being involved in a participatory research study. The dearth of personal reflective accounts may be because participatory research predominantly focuses on accomplishing practical and social justice goals that transcend individual learning and needs. Participatory research is very much about making a difference in the real world at a collective level, rather aiming to facilitate the researcher's growth and development.

An insightful reflective account by Southby (2017) reviews their experience of conducting participatory research, at PhD level, into the potential for football fandom to be a route to social inclusion for people with a learning disability. As well as drawing on similar accounts written by other participatory researchers. This paper identifies a number of recurring themes through the course of the study, in particular, the tension between have a sense of being an expert in control of the research process and versus a wish to be open to the contributions offered by participants. Williams (2020) also describes the experience of being a PhD researcher (in this case, with a focus on language and loneliness in people living with autism) who is pulled in the direction of conforming to established expert-driven research procedures while at the same time being aware of the huge potential added value of adopting a more participatory approach. Blakley (2022) explores the stress and personal learning arising from the ethical approval stage of a participatory research proposal, specifically around a growing appreciation that what, in the end, was most helpful was to be willing to be guided by the detailed personal knowledge-by-experience of service user co-researchers.

A study by Lenette et al. (2019) reported on a collaborative reflexive project in which seven participatory researchers at different stages in their research careers, met to document and make sense of the challenges associated with this type of work. Important themes in their discussion were the extent to which participatory research is misunderstood and undervalued in universities, possibly because it is mainly carried out by women, and difficulties in negotiating relationships and maintaining professional boundaries. Demers et al. (2022) wrote about the challenges faced by community-based participatory researchers moving to a new job in a university in another part of the country, particularly around the intensive and exhausting networking and trust-building required to establish potential research collaborations.

Some studies have explored the experiences of non-researcher (i.e., service user) participants in research (Dirik et al., 2018; Jones and Hunt, 2022; Lea et al., 2020; Lindquist-Grantz et al., 2022). Although participants described challenges around understanding some of the technical language used by university-based researchers, and sometimes found it hard to have their voices heard during meetings, the overall consensus across these studies was that involvement in research was interesting, personally rewarding, and meaningful. Dirik et al. (2018) provide a detailed account of the sometimes difficult process through which professional researchers and service user participants were able to come together as a cohesive and productive working group. A contrasting perspective on non-researcher involvement can be found in a paper written by three film-makers who worked together to produce a portrayal of grief and loss that was partly informed by their own life experience and partly guided by material from interviews with practitioners in various areas of bereavement practice and inputs from actors and technical production staff (Dawson et al., 2021). Each of the three individuals at the centre of this project was profoundly affected by the degree to which their involvement in this arts-based collaborative inquiry process opened up painful unresolved personal memories. A sense of participatory research being personally "unsettling" has also been reported by Beeker et al. (2022) and von Peter and Bos (2022).

An analysis of the emotional meaning of participatory research by Klocker (2015) suggests that a common burden associated with this kind of work is the experience of failure. Many projects seek to bring about change in relation to practices that are deeply entrenched in existing organisational and societal norms and systems. As a result, it may not be realistic to expect long-lasting benefits to participants.

Other writers have described how engaging in participatory research has facilitated transformational learning. For example, academic researchers who have worked with co-researchers from Indigenous communities have described arriving at a new appreciation of the meaning of spirituality (Barnes et al., 2017) and the significance of land and country (Country et al., 2020, 2022; Hernández et al, 2021). Service user members of research teams report significant person learning through training in research skills (Blair et al., 2022).

A large-scale study of personal outcomes in community-based participatory research partnerships: was carried out by Espinosa et al. (2020). What they found was that research participants reported a wide range of benefits at a personal level, including becoming more confident, expanding their knowledge and understanding, and feeling more comfortable expressing opinions. Participants also described many ways that they had become better able to function in colleague relationships and groups. There were also many examples of how being a co-researcher had led to being able to get a better job, and entering or re-entering education. This study did not address the possible incidence of negative or disappointing personal outcomes.

There have been several studies of the experiences of therapy practitioner involvement in collaborative Practice Research Network (PRN) projects. Useful starting points for accessing this literature are Castonguay et al. (2010) and Bartholomew et al. (2017).

Conclusions

The primary function of participatory research is to generate new understanding and social justice outcomes in relation to problematic aspects of community life. However, such research also has an effect on the lives of those who are involved. This chapter has examined the participatory research process from the perspective of individual outcomes and experiences rather than collective or project-level outputs. It can be seen that involvement in participatory research can effect individuals in many different ways, ranging from gains in skills and confidence, through to transformational learning that upends the person's personal equilibrium or their way of seeing the world.

Responding ethically to the personal challenges and opportunities associated with research participation requires attention to what the study might mean to each individual member of a research team, and designing the study in a way that allows that personal trajectory to be supported in a caring way. Across the studies highlighted in this chapter, the most common way of offering this kind of support has been to build in time for group meetings at which participants could share their feelings around their participation in the team. There was also a strong emphasis on creating a positive group culture, so that all relationships and interactions can be as constructive as possible.

Studies where therapy clients or former clients are co-researchers present particular ethical challenges in respect of personal impacts. Therapy clients are persons with strengths, and are able to make their own decision whether or not to engage with a research project. Nevertheless, it is essential to allow that choice to be as informed as possible, by making it clear at the recruitment stage what the time, narrative, emotional and dialogical aspects of a participatory study are likely to involve. It is also important to build opportunities for one-to-one support, including for anyone who decides to leave a project because its demands have become too intense.

The study by Matheson and Weightman (2021a, 2021b) into the therapy experiences of clients suffering from complex post-traumatic stress disorder, provides a valuable model for how researchers can facilitate participatory research in a manner that both takes account of potential vulnerabilities, and provides a framework for positive growth and recovery. Matheson and Weightman (2021b) designed their study so that it sat alongside other post-therapy training and recovery activities and support available to participants. They made sure that there were regular opportunities for participants to de-brief and reflect together, around their research experience, and created a procedure for the researchers themselves to monitor what was happening in the group, and process their own responses. A particularly noteworthy aspect of this study, described in Matheson and Weightman (2021b), was the way in which the researchers offered a secure, safe and explicit frame or structure for the group, while being open to participant control of what happened within that structure, for instance in relation to the interview strategy and data analysis. The approach taken by Matheson and Weightman (2021a, 2021b) can be seen as reflecting an appreciation of the significance and relevance of both caring and empowering leadership responsibilities of academic researchers.

Topics for reflection and discussion

1 In relation to a participatory therapy study that you might carry out yourself, what do you think might be the opportunities for personal learning and development that it might offer for participants? What might be the areas of vulnerability for participants? How might you explain these potential opportunities and risks, at the point of recruiting participants?
2 At the heart of participatory therapy research, there exists a process through which a group of people with different backgrounds, needs and interests, meet together to explore emotionally and interpersonally complex issues of human relationships. How does the group need to be organised and facilitated, to enable that process

to unfold in a productive and life-enhancing manner? Based on your own knowledge of group therapy theory and dynamics, and your own personal experience in groups, what are the skills and concepts that you bring to this task?

3 In a participatory research study, how can academic researchers and non-academic or community members of a research team work together to look after members of the group during episodes of personal vulnerability or crisis?
4 The focus of the present chapter has been primarily on personal outcomes for clients, service users, carers, and members of the public who are involved in participatory research. In what ways might the personal outcomes for practitioner co-researchers (e.g., in the context of a collective autoethnography project, or a Practitioner Research Network) be different, from outcomes experienced by service user participants, and how could they be most effectively accommodated? In reflecting on this topic, it can be helpful to focus on a specific example of study (either a published study, or a study that you intend to carry out) rather than thinking about it the issues in more general terms.

Chapter 8

Methodological innovation and flexibility

Harnessing courage, imagination, and openness to learning

Introduction

The field of counselling and psychotherapy research, as well as the broader psychotherapeutic research literature, has been dominated by studies that collect data through standardised procedures, such as quantitative measures and questionnaires, or (in qualitative research) pre-determined interview schedules and formalised data analysis techniques. Standardised data collection procedures, in many instances backed up by extensive research that has established their validity and reliability, make it easier for studies to be replicated, and for findings across different studies to be compared. As a consequence, the use of such procedures has come to be regarded as an essential aspect of the credibility of a study. University-based researchers in counselling, psychotherapy and mental health, have generally received expensive training in the development and application of such procedures. Those conducting systematic reviews of research are likely to exclude studies that have not employed standardised methods of data collection and analysis.

Participatory research inevitably creates a situation in which the relevance of standardised measures is brought into question. Participatory planning of a research study opens up the possibility that service users, consumers, and general public participants may object to a questionnaire or rating scale on the grounds that it is not sensitive to important aspects of their experience of the phenomenon being investigated. They may suggest other ways of collecting and analysing data that make more sense to them. This kind of conversation is part of the territory of participatory research. A commitment to epistemic justice means that professional researchers cannot justify the inclusion of a data collection technique solely on the grounds that it fulfils academic criteria of reliability and validity. Rather, epistemic justice requires a willingness to engage in dialogue that takes account of the everyday knowledge of research participants. As a result, participatory research is associated with many different kinds of methodological innovation, encompassing the invention of new methods, flexible adaptation of established procedures, and studies in which the boundary between active therapeutic intervention (and other practical outcomes) and data collection are intentionally blurred.

DOI: 10.4324/9781003405818-9

To facilitate methodological flexibility and innovation, all those taking part in a participatory study need to be resourceful, in the sense of being open to ideas and techniques from other disciplines or that exist in the wider community or culture as a whole, and also willing to engage in open dialogue and shared decision-making around the pros and cons of novel, adapted or improvised techniques. At an underlying ethical level, participatory research calls for moral courage and imagination. Courage is required for service users and consumer members of a research team to be willing to speak out against research tools that may have been used in large number of published studies in high status research journals – techniques through which the professional researcher members of the team may have made their reputations. The stakes are also high for professional researcher members of a team, because they will be well aware of the implications, in terms of negative reactions from researcher colleagues or their university hierarchy, of deviating from the path of methodological convention. This kind of innovation also call for moral imagination, in the form of anticipating the potential for both personal harm and benefit that might arise from the use of an untested approach to data collection.

The present chapter discusses a range of examples of methodological innovation and flexibility in the field of participatory research on psychotherapeutic practice, in relation to the ethical rationale for the approach that was taken, and the ethical procedures that were adopted to safeguard participant rights and wellbeing.

Forms of methodological innovation

Methodological innovation is a thread that runs through the entire participatory research literature. It is not possible to offer a comprehensive review of all of the many different ways in which research teams have tackled this issue. Instead, methodological flexibility is explored in relation to a set of broad categories: augmented interview techniques; the use of writing; participatory therapy outcome studies; co-produced single-case studies; theatre methods; and, participant involvement in qualitative data analysis. Additional examples of adaptable data collection tools that have been used in studies in many countries can be found in the *Participatory research toolkit* created by Sood et al. (2018).

Augmented interview techniques

Studies in which a sample of clients or service users are interviewed by a researcher, in order to explore the informant's lived experience, ways of coping, and views about services, have made a valuable contribution to the enhancement of health and social care for several decades. This kind of qualitative research gives a voice to consumers of care, in a form that allows practitioners and policymakers to take better account of what they want and need from professional providers. In an important sense, one of the key motivations for the development of participatory research in these fields has been the recognition that, while the traditional, largely expert-driven, use of qualitative research methods does not adequately do justice to the reality of the lives of those who are studied. So, although this type of research is on the whole oriented towards social justice goals (i.e., giving service users and members of marginalised groups a chance to tell their story), in some instances can have the opposite effect, by interpreting these stories from a professional or theoretical perspective, or not capturing key threads in such stories. Participatory methods therefore represent an ethical step forward, by giving consumers, service users and members of the public even more of a say in, and control over, how a study is carried out.

In conventional qualitative research, data are typically collected through semi-structured interviews designed and administered by the researcher. From the perspective of non-researcher participants, there are at least two major drawbacks to this approach. First, the interviewee (often a vulnerable person, or someone from a marginalised group) is meeting with a researcher who is from a different background to them, and who may be experienced by them as a symbol or representative of those in authority who have treated them badly in the past. They may find it hard to trust the researcher, understand their questions, or have a sense that the researcher really gets what they are telling them. A further difficulty is that providing a rational and focused account of relevant aspects of their lives, within a limited block of time, may be a hard thing to do. It may be hard because the life experience that is being explored is somewhat jumbled and fragmented and not easily rendered in a linear form. Or the events are associated with, or trigger, emotional responses that the person may struggle to put into words, or may not want to convey at all. Or interview questions that invite generalised responses may conflict with the person's sense that the issues being asked about are inextricably tied to specific concrete times and places.

For these reasons, many participatory studies have devised ways of adapting interview methodology in order to make it more meaningful for informants. In relation to one-off recorded interviews, widely used approaches to augmenting or enhancing the interview process include involving participants in the design of the interview schedule, piloting the interview on and with participants, holding interviews at a place chosen by the interviewee, providing interview questions in advance, having the interview carried out by a participant rather than by an academic researcher, encouraging the interviewee to switch off the microphone at points when they would prefer to talk off the record, and building in a second interview or consult to enable the informant to add further thoughts that had occurred to them following the first interview or to allow the interviewer to clarify aspects of what was said on that earlier occasion. Each of these strategies brings its own ethical dilemmas that require consideration and discussion with a research team, and transparency in relation to ethics approval committees. For example, holding an interview in a public place raises questions about participant privacy and confidentiality and researcher safety, and interviews conducted by participants raise questions about such matters as the capacity of the interviewer to handle informant distress, or interviewer understanding of confidentiality boundaries. None of these ethical issues are insurmountable – they have all been successfully negotiated in previous studies – but they need to be carefully discussed, with appropriate procedures agreed and documented, and any necessary training made available. In terms of approval from an ethics committee, IRB or other stakeholder group, the fact that service user/consumer participants have been involved in formulating solutions to ethical issues, can be reassuring (see, for example, Blakley, 2022).

Other responses to perceived limitations of conventional researcher-administered verbal interviews have involved the augmentation of talk with different types of visual, embodied, and contextualised activities, such as the use of mapping, photography, and walking.

Mapping. Many of the earliest examples of participatory research were carried out in Indigenous and marginalised communities with the aim of supporting people to argue for, and create, satisfactory housing conditions, transport networks and ways of making a living, or to justify land use and ownership. Research participants suggested that a valuable means of collecting information in these contexts was to invite local people to construct maps of the country or territory with which they lived, as a means of anchoring conversations about the meaning of different places (Cornwall & Jewkes, 1995). Over time, the use of mapping in participatory research (and more widely in qualitative research as a whole) expanded to include body mapping (De Jager et al., 2016; Klein & Milner, 2019; Skop, 2016) and concept mapping (Adams et al., 2021). Body mapping, where a research participant might draw a full-size outline of their body and then fill it in, using words and colours to indicate emotions and meanings associated with that body area, is a particularly valuable technique in relation to research on psychotherapeutic practice, because it provides a tangible means of investigating and making a record of processes and experiences that are highly relevant to therapy and recovery (Boydell et al., 2018).

Photography. Photographs taken by research participants to capture significant scenes, places and relationships, are another strategy for augmenting research interviews that has been in use for many decades (Wang & Burris, 1994). More recently, this approach has been described as *photovoice*: research participants take photographs about places, people or objects that are meaningful for them, and then talk about these images in an individual interview or in a group setting (Courcy & Koniou, 2024; Doroud et al., 2022; Sitter, 2017; Woodgate et al., 2017). Typically, a standard method of qualitative data analysis, such as thematic analysis, is used to identify meanings expressed by participants, with article structured around a mix of themes, quotes, and images. In some situations, it is possible to extend the photovoice process into exhibitions in which selected photographs are publicly exhibited, accompanied by commentaries written or spoken by participants. A large number of photovoice studies have been published – it represents a data collection approach that is meaningful, enjoyable, evocative, and potentially therapeutic for participants, as well as having the potential to disseminate findings in a form that can have a strong impact on audiences. A data collection approach that extends the possibilities of photovoice is participatory film-making (Baumann et al., 2020, 2024).

Walking. The experience of walking together, while an interview or research conversation is being conducted, enables the research participant to feel more at ease, and to have more control in relation to the direction of both the discussion and the journey. Walking frees the speaker from the direct gaze of the questioner. It also allows important aspects of self to be conveyed through action rather than through words, such as the connection between the informant and various places and persons encountered during a walk. For those involved in participatory research, talking interviews may represent a valuable adjunct or replacement for seated face-to-face meetings (Kinney, 2017, 2021; Lenette, 2021; Marcotte et al., 2022).

Mapping, photovoice, and walking are each associated with ethical issues that need to be considered. In particular, there exists a substantial literature around the ethics of photovoice (McDonald & Capous-Desyllas, 2021; Pichon et al. 2022) regarding the possibility that images of particular places may trigger upsetting memories, threats to confidentiality when photographs are displayed in articles and exhibitions, consent from other people captured in photographs, and the question of whether the photographer should be named if an exhibition is held. These data collection techniques hold a special synergy and resonance for many psychotherapeutic practitioner-researchers, because they are also increasingly deployed as techniques within various types of therapeutic intervention.

Writing

Open-ended and expressive writing is a data collection approach that has been incorporated into several participatory studies of psychotherapeutic practice. One type of writing that has been widely used in both psychotherapeutic and wider social science research has been the use of solicited diaries (Mackrill, 2007, 2008a). In this type of study, the research participants invited to keep a diary in relation to events and experiences suggested by the primary researcher, but is free to write in whatever style, or at whatever length, they see as appropriate for them. Any study of this kind can be viewed as participatory given that it involves ongoing commitment and effort by the participant, as well as continuing reflection and decision-making around their choice of what to write about what to omit. Unlike archival diary studies, based on diaries kept by a person for their own use, a solicited diary study is also participatory in the sense that the person knows from the start that they are writing for a specific, scientific purpose. An example of a carefully documented participatory diary study was an investigation by Mackrill (2007, 2008b.c, 2011) in which therapists and clients kept regular diaries over the course of their work together. In addition to their involvement in creating the data (i.e., diary entries), participants also engaged in dialogue with the researcher around his analysis and interpretation of what they had written. Other examples of the use of writing in participatory psychotherapeutic research include a study by Beck et al. (2005) that took a dialogal phenomenological approach to understanding therapist experiences of despair, collaborative writing studies by Etherington (2000, 2002, 2003) around client and therapist narratives of their experiences of trauma, life-story group writing research by Lieblich (2013), and collective autoethnographic writing studies of aspects of psychotheraputic learning and development by Asfeldt and Beames (2017), Van Katwyk and Seko (2017), Råbu et al. (2021), Speciale et al. (2015), and Yang et al. (2022).

Significant methodological commonalities across these studies include the personal meaningfulness for participants of engaging in writing, and the open-endedness of the inquiry process: writing about an area experience of experience triggered reflection on that experience, which in turn lead to more writing. In most studies, writing was combined with some kind of group discussion (or, in the case of Van Katwyk & Seko, 2017, group dance). Although writing-based participatory research projects are necessarily selective, because not everyone who has a story to tell will be comfortable with writing it down, this approach seems to be capable of generating intensive participation over considerable periods of time. An important ethical issue in this kind of work involves the vulnerability of writing about painful experiences on one's own – many of the studies commented on the necessity to establish supportive relationships between members of a writing group, linked to ongoing informal contact by phone and email. A further ethical issue is that in some of the studies cited above (e.g., autoethnographic projects), those writing about life experience are also named as authors of articles and reports that are subsequently published – which makes it hard to maintain confidentiality.

Using theatre

Interviews, writing, and other data collection methods such as questionnaires, primarily function by inviting the research participant to retrospectively describe aspects of their experience. The process of providing such an account also inevitably includes some degree of reflection, interpretation, or justification in respect of the experiences and events that are being recalled. These methods are not so effective in capturing what happens between people, or the immediate bodily felt experience that accompanies all action. In the light of such methodological limitations, some participatory studies have used live theatrical enactment of scenes from social life, as a means of exploring both relational process and implicit emotional meanings.

A closely described example of how theatre can be used in participatory research can be found in a project based in Denmark (Ammentorp et al., 2018; Larsen et al., 2018). This study was carried out with staff in a major hospital that was already committed to the use of shared decision-making between patients and their nurses or doctors, across all aspects of clinical care. It became apparent, to some clinicians and also within the staff training group, that the evidence-based model of shared decision-making skills that was being used in the hospital was not sufficient to handle situations in which the decision being made touched on existential issues for the patient, such as the meaning of their life, acceptance of death, or hope for the future. A programme of participatory research, involving nurses, doctors, patients and relatives/carers, was initiated in order to develop an enhanced training programme. A key element in the study was the use of theatre workshops, in which trained actors played out brief doctor-patient-nurse scenarios that were watched by groups of patients and carers, and by groups of health care practitioners. The workshops included opportunities for participants to suggest other ways in which the scenario might unfold (e.g., other things that the doctor might have said) and then to look at how the scene played out differently. Workshops also included time for reflection in small groups, around reactions to the theatre episodes. Researchers facilitated these processes, kept notes of themes that emerged, and collected additional responses through questionnaires. An analysis of findings from the overall study is available in Ammentorp et al. (2018), and a more detailed account of the theatre workshops can be found in Larsen et al. (2018). The authors of the study found that the insights generated by the theatre workshops (and then incorporated into training and supervision) lead to a decisive shift in the approach to shared decision-making in the hospital. In particular staff learned to embrace the idea that, to explore the personal existential meaning of a healthcare decision for a patient with a serious condition, they needed to be willing and able to draw on, and appropriately share, their own personal feelings and life experiences that were relevant to (or evoked by) the choices open to the patient. Examples of what this looked like in practice are available in Gregersen et al. (2022) and Prinds et al. (2021).

A series of studies of life challenges and accomplishments of young people from Indigenous communities in Canada, used theatre as a means of capturing key meanings and experiences in participants (Camargo Plazas et al., 2019; Conrad, 2020, 2023).

Theatre has also been used as a participatory methodology in the dissemination stage of such studies, for instance when material from interviews are turned into a stage play. Examples of this approach can be found in Hundt et al. (2019), Lieblich (2006) and Råbu et al. (2021). The process of transforming interview texts into a play is highly participatory, because it will usually involve inputs from many different perspectives, such as that of the playwright, director, set designer and actors, in dialogue with researchers. Often this includes participation by those who were interviewed in the first place, for example around the acceptability to them of how they are portrayed, and in relation to maintaining anonymity when long sections of their interview transcript are used (see, for example, Råbu et al., 2021). In some studies, audiences at a research-based theatrical production may be invited to discuss their responses to what they have seen, thus allowing a further layer of participatory inquiry to take place.

There are several ways in which looking at an aspect of social life as a drama can be relevant to the accomplishment of social justice goals, and other research purposes. Unlike other research methods, such as interviews or questionnaires, that produce a predominantly detached, reflective, cognitive and fixed account of experience, watching or participating in a drama, or other forms of enactment, such as comedy (Caslin et al., 2022), creates opportunities for more emotional, embodied, imaginative and metaphoric ways of knowing. Not only are audiences more likely to personally engage with a play, compared to reading an article, they are also likely to spend more time with the material, which leads to the possibility of developing an understanding that is more memorable and nuanced. Finally, as in the Ammentorp et al. (2018) study, there may be opportunities to re-enact what has happened, in the form of trying out different responses that might have different outcomes – this can be useful in terms of transferring learning from a study, into practice.

Participants choosing how they want to tell their story

Some participatory studies have taken the view that individuals being interviewed may have preferences around how they might want to share personal information, in terms of which research activities and techniques with which they feel most comfortable or that give them the best opportunity to express themselves. In a participatory study of sexual health in young people in Kenya, Chubb et al. (2022) found that participants preferred to talk about their views and experiences in the context of a *baraza* – an Indigenous East African format for community meetings. In their study exploring the experiences of children who had been victims of domestic abuse, Beetham et al. (2019) and Gabriel et al. (2017) used as 'child-centred' interview approach that offered participants a range of arts-based communications formats: photographs, video clips, a secret box, drawing activities and mind-mapping. In a programme of participatory research into the experiences of young people who had received dramatherapy, Cedar et al. (2022) and Jones et al. (2020) similarly offered the choice of an array of arts and drama-based (e.g., puppets) as vehicles for facilitating research conversations. They also used play and creative strategies to help participants differentiate between therapy sessions and research time. Brubacher et al. (2021) found that collective sewing groups were congenial settings for research with Inuit women. In these studies, the use of different communication formats does not compromise the underlying research process – the aim is to generate a rich interview text that can be analysed.

Further examples of methodological flexibility and improvisation are outlined by Lambert and Carr (2018) in their participatory study of the mental health needs of women. In this study, participants took the initiative by insisting on taking decisions that went far beyond the research protocol. For instance, during a focus group session, participants insisted that everyone who had turned up (a number substantially higher than had been approved in the ethics protocol) would meet as one large group. Also, during the group meetings, participants phoned other people who they believed might have something useful to add to the ongoing discussion, and invited them to come to the meeting room and join in.

In a participatory study that aimed to empower mothers living in challenging circumstances, Groot et al. (2021) found that, as they developed more trust and confidence, members of the group pushed for more emotionally expressive, arts-based methods to be used to capture their stories. In the Rouse et al. (2015) study of therapist creativity, participants conveyed the personal meaning of the project through a group exhibition of their own original art work.

Reading between the lines, it is often possible to identify evidence of data collection flexibility in studies that do not necessarily highlight this aspect of their methodology.

For example, in many participatory (and other) studies, informants are given choices around the location and length of an interview. In their reflection on a participatory study that they conducted with disabled young people, Goodley and Runswick-Cole (2012) describe how they came to understand that this kind of methodological flexibility represented ethical good practice: many of the young people with whom they were working actively resisted what they perceived as the intrusiveness of any attempt to observe them or directly question them.

Co-produced case studies

Case studies that document and analyse how the process of therapy unfolds over the course of treatment, or provide an in-depth analysis of the outcome of therapy in a single case, represent a significant and growing source of evidence in relation to counselling and psychotherapy theory and practice (McLeod, 2022). The majority of therapy single-case studies are carried out and written up from the perspective of either the therapist, or a team of researchers. Few such studies include interviews with clients, and even fewer involve clients in the design of the study, collection and analysis of data, or writing-up.

There are significant ethical challenges associated with client active participation in a case study project. For example, such involvement may open up emotional wounds and lead to unclear boundaries between conversations that are intended to be therapeutic, and those that are aimed at generating a research output. As a consequence, such studies call for considerable ethical sensitivity and maturity on the part of the practitioner-researcher. Examples of co-produced therapy case studies arising from a joint inquiry process between client and therapist include Blunden (2020), Etherington (2000), and Yalom and Elkin (2008).

Measuring the outcomes of psychotherapeutic interventions

A substantial proportion of research studies into the effectiveness of counselling and psychotherapy – and other approaches to helping individuals and families – is based on the administration of self-report symptom measures at the start and finish of therapy, and where possible also at follow-up. Historically, this form of research has been highly expert-driven, with both the measures themselves, and procedures for collecting data, being guided by strict guidelines around what is considered to be best practice. As discussed in Chapter 1, a growing set of participatory studies have explored issues around how outcome studies can be carried out in a manner consistent with the interests and values of service users and frontline practitioners. Participatory methods have also been employed in the development of user-designed outcome measures. Given the high academic and scientific status accorded to controlled experimental research designs and rigorous measurement within disciplines such as psychology and psychiatry, the adoption of an alternative research strategy, grounded in participatory methodology, has required a significant degree of courage.

Qualitative data analysis

Most participatory studies make use of qualitative methods of data analysis, such as thematic analysis or a grounded theory approach, to identify patterns of meaning in information collected in interviews, focus groups or written documents such as diaries. When the process of analysis is carried out on a collective basis by a team of co-researchers that includes a mix of individuals with academic backgrounds and others with expert by experience backgrounds, it is inevitable that the procedure will diverge from what is outlined in recommended in the relevant data analysis textbook. For example, following individual interviews with women survivors of sexual abuse, Morrow and Smith (1995) invited informants to be part of a data analysis group that worked together for several weeks. Although the analysis was based on a grounded theory approach, it is clear that what actually happened went beyond anything that would be possible for a solo-grounded theory researcher, or even within an analysis group consisting of only trained researchers, in relation to the added layers of meaning brought to the task by the survivor co-researchers.

Levitt et al. (2021) discussed the challenges associated with any group-based consensus approach to analysing qualitative data and possible strategies for addressing these dilemmas. They point out that an increasing proportion of qualitative researchers – whether they adopt a formal participatory/co-production approach or not – make use of some kind of additional scrutiny of the data analysis process. This is because such strategies as independent auditing, or member checking (informants commenting on whether the analysis makes sense to them) are highlighted within widely accepted general criteria for rigour in qualitative research. Following their review of existing strategies for achieving consensus in group-based methods of analysis, Levitt et al. (2021) suggest that none of the currently available approaches effectively tackle the issue of epistemic justice – the likelihood that the views of higher status members of the research team are likely to dominate the analytic process.

Levitt et al. (2021) make several recommendations for enhancing the quality of collective analysis of qualitative data. They suggest that, before analysis commences, all members of the team should talk about the specific forms of expertise that they bring to the task. For example, an academic researcher member may have knowledge of research methodology, while citizen or service user members may possess knowledge of a variety of everyday life facets of the topic being investigated. The aim here is to ensure that the cultural positions and identities represented within the team are given equal weight and status. They also propose that research groups should be willing to learn from, and be guided by structures for group decision-making that exist within Indigenous cultures, such as *aajiiqatigiingniq* (Ferrazzi et al., 2019), listening with the heart (Polansky et al., 2022), "what touched your heart?" (Hallett et al., 2017), and sharing circles (Waddell et al., 2021; Waddell-Henowitch et al., 2022). Characteristic features of these approaches are the deep respect, and amount of time, given to each participant, and a willingness to wait for a shared understanding to emerge within the group. There is also close attention paid to the bodily, felt experience evoked by the person speaking, or by a transcript that is being read. Hess et al. (2022) published a report that provides a detailed account of how such an approach to collective analysis of qualitative data unfolded within a participatory study of the experiences of Latina/x immigrants in the US. In addition to the strategies outlined by Levitt et al. (2021) they found that they needed blocks of time, in the form of retreat meetings, to allow research team members to get to know each other. They also found that conducting the analysis in the preferred language of team members (for the majority of their group, this was Spanish) significantly enhanced the depth of analysis, even if it involved time-consuming and awkward simultaneous translation within session.

Locock et al. (2019) and Sweeney et al. (2013) explored the process of inviting UK service users to contribute to the analysis of qualitative data. These studies found that people without previous research training or experience were able to engage with this task with limited preparation. Although themes identified by service users tended to fall broadly along the same lines as themes identified by experienced researchers, the former were also able to pick up on details and implicit meanings that had not been apparent to the latter, in some instances adding significant depth to the analysis. The majority of service user researchers in these projects enjoyed this work, and found it meaningful and interesting.

A further consideration in relation to the analysis of qualitative data by members of a research team, is that, at least in some circumstances, new, or more nuanced and differentiated, understanding arises through attention to differences in how material is interpreted by different members of the group, and to different voices or positions within the material itself (Soggiu et al., 2021). This process can be seen as involving a willingness to take account of micro-examples of epistemic privilege, rather than focusing only on more visible dimensions of power and privilege associated with status and experience. Guidelines around alternative strategies for engaging service users in collaborative analysis of qualitative interview transcripts have been produced by Jennings et al. (2018).

Ethical implications of methodological flexibility

Research that is responsive to the diversity of styles of self-reflection and communication preferred by participants, inevitable involves flexibility and innovation around methods of data collection and analysis. Schoonenboom (2024) has described the use of different research tools and methodologies as comprising ways of performing different ways of knowing.

It is crucial that the kind of open-ness to improvisation and creativity explored in the present chapter, does not take place at the expense of participants. For example, in situations where potentially emotionally powerful activities are being utilised, such as art-making, theatre and diary-keeping, it is necessary that the possibility of harmful experiences is carefully considered, and strategies for limiting and remedying risk are put in place. Groot et al. (2021) give an example of the distress caused to members of one participatory project, arising from press coverage (and misrepresentation) of artwork that had been created by the group. In a reflective account of the experience of carrying out a theatre-based participatory study with young people, Conrad (2022) concluded that the single most important factor in the eventual success of the project was consistent attention and responsiveness to ethical issues.

A useful discussion of the kind of practical ethical work that may need to take place around methodological innovation and flexibility can be found in a paper by Pavarini et al. (2021) outlining their learning around addressing ethical issues when using participatory arts methods in co-produced research young people with adverse childhood experiences. This research team identified a wide range of issues that they needed to deal with, in relation to working this potentially highly vulnerable group. They emphasised the importance of careful planning and co-design at the start of a project, to make sure that everyone knew what was going to happen, what the possible sensitive topics and activities might be, how to communicate discomfort, and how to respond appropriately in such situations. An example of a practical technique employed by this team (and other participatory researchers) is to agree on a physical object that can be present in the room (or equivalent in an online meeting or interview) that can be used to signal discomfort. This could be a clock dial where hand could be adjusted to point to 'OK', 'slow down' or 'stop, I need time out' (or whatever signals are deemed relevant within a particular project setting). Alternatively, items of different colour could be used, such as green block to indicate that things are fine, and a red block to indicate stop. Such physical signalling systems can make it easier for any participant (service user or researcher) to communicate their wishes and feelings at a moment when it may be hard for them to speak, or they silence themselves for fear of interrupting someone else who is speaking. A similar technique is to encourage all participants to design their own badges that convey how they are on that day. For these kinds of strategies to be effective, there needs to be a shared understanding of what will happen when a participant wants to slow down or take time out, including provision of a suitable space where the person might take themselves.

Such signalling systems, accompanied by shared understanding of their purpose, create conditions of safety and care within which participants can engage in potentially upsetting activities and conversations. A further type of ethics work that is involved in the use of flexible and innovative research methods is centred on the willingness to act with courage. The concept of courage is multi-faceted, and courage can be expressed in different ways in different situations, such as bold actions at a moment in time, or ongoing fortitude. Courage is generally understood as a response to a challenging situation that is oriented towards some type of common good rather than being driven by self-interest. Courage typically calls for a willingness to enter into feelings of fear, anxiety, dread and ambiguity, rather than avoiding or deflecting such experiences. Studies of what people say about acting with courage in professional contexts suggest that such episodes can often be associated with a dread of the potential consequences of behaving authentically and honestly in ways that may violate or transcend professional rules and boundaries or theoretical assumptions (see, for example, Goto et al., 2022). This type of courage is clearly very relevant for researchers – particularly novice or junior researchers – who may have concerns about how their approach may be judged by colleagues who position themselves within more expert-driven research traditions. A further important aspect of courage as a strand of ethics work in participatory research is that the service user participants in a study may have more first-hand experience of courage than the academic researchers. Individuals who have lived with an illness or disability, or who belong within a marginalised or oppressed community or cultural group, generally have ample experience of everyday courage, fortitude and patience (Finfgeld, 1999). Willingness to make use of such life experiences to benefit others, by being involved in participatory or co-produced research, can itself require considerable courage.

Conclusions

Methodological innovation is an intrinsic aspect of participatory research: co-researchers who do not have prior knowledge and experience around standard methods for data collection and analysis inevitably have their own ideas about these processes that they feed into the research decision-making process. Ideas and activities suggested by clients, service users, and other community participants can make a powerful contribution to a study, by engaging participant imagination and depth of emotional involvement. At the same time, however, they may have unintended consequences in relation confidentiality and risk of harm. Making sure that methodological innovation is carried out in a constructive fashion, involves active commitment to detailed ethics work, in the context of a caring and supportive research team culture in which honest feedback is encouraged around what is helpful or not helpful for all concerned. This is also an area of ethical practice in which sharing of ethical learning is important. For example, within longer-established innovative methodologies such as photovoice, it has been possible to build up an extensive shared understanding of where the risks might lie, and how to address them.

Topics for reflection and discussion

1 Identify a participatory research study, on a specific topic, that you would like to carry out. What procedures for data collection would you want to use? What kind of extensions to these procedures, or alternative procedures, could you envisage being suggested by co-researchers in your team? How might you respond to their suggestions, in terms of arriving at an agreement on whether to implement them or not (or adapt them in some way)? What kind of consultation might need to take place with your research sponsor, funder or supervisor, or the ethics committee/IRB that approved the study proposal? How might you write the ethics proposal in a way that allowed space for this kind of methodological flexibility?
2 Choose any one of the creative methodologies that have been widely used in participatory research, such as theatre, expressive arts, writing, or use of photography/

video. Either in relation to a published study that is of interest to you, *or* to a study you would hope to carry out yourself, what were (or could be) the ethical challenges associated with that technique, and how were they (could they be) addressed?

3 You are conducting a participatory research study in which people who have received therapy are being interviewed by members of a research team consisting mainly of service users. In an early meeting of the team, someone suggests that it might be a good idea to offer to conduct interviews in outdoor settings, such as walking along a beach. How do you collectively decide on how to conduct outdoor interviews in an ethically safe, respectful, and sensitive manner?
4 Historically, starting from case studies published by Freud, case-based knowledge has made an enormous contribution to therapy training and practice. Co-produced case studies, carried out by the client and therapist (and perhaps others) working together, have the potential to take this type of research evidence to another level. If you were a member of a research ethics committee or IRB, what would you want to see in an ethics proposal that would reassure you that such a project safeguarded the rights and wellbeing of both the client and the therapist?

Chapter 9

Implications and learning for therapy practice

Introduction

This book has used examples of participatory research in the field of counselling, psychotherapy, recovery, and related areas, to demonstrate how ethical pluralism and active engagement in ethics work can make a contribution to practical justice. Involvement in participatory, collaborative, and co-produced research provides both therapy trainees and experienced practitioners with significant opportunities for learning about processes that are also central to therapy practice, such as dialogue, shared decision-making, and the functioning of power, control, difference, and privilege. Such involvement also provides opportunities for gaining a deeper appreciation of the meaning of broad moral and ethical themes, such as care, solidarity, and justice, in the context of professional relationships. This closing chapter explores how these forms of ethical awareness and ethics work can translate into increased resourcefulness as a therapy practitioner and the design and operation of therapy service provision.

The significance of a pluralistic ethical stance

A central aim of this book has been to highlight the idea of pluralistic ethics. The concept of pluralistic ethics refers to an understanding that we live our lives within a multi-faceted moral and ethical order that underpins everything we do. A fundamental characteristic of being a person is that one has a sense of right and wrong. Acting in ways that are wrong, or being subjected to such actions, has a deep and enduring effect on well-being, mental health, bodily functioning, relationships, and connectedness with the more-than-human world. Most of us, in advanced industrial societies, live in a world in which the ethical and moral order is fragmented: different people hold different ideas about what is right or wrong. As a consequence, there are many situations where it is not clear what would be the right thing to do. There is also an absence of a shared language for talking about moral and ethical matters.

Counselling, psychotherapy, and related psychotherapeutic activities, can be seen as practical justice – ways of getting life back on the 'right' path, or repairing relationships that have been damaged by injustice. In a similar fashion, moral values permeate

DOI: 10.4324/9781003405818-10

research on counselling and psychotherapy. For example, therapy researchers have used different implicit moral assumptions when developing ways of evaluating the outcomes of therapy: Is the purpose of therapy to reduce symptoms so that the individual can be economically productive? Or to feel that they are entitled to fulfil themselves, seek pleasure, and enjoy life? Or to be more eco-aware and politically active?

Pluralistic ethics is a standpoint that acknowledges that contemporary life comprises multiple cultural traditions that emphasise different values and ethical priorities. To be able to operate ethically within a professional role – such as being a therapist, or being a researcher – it is therefore necessary to be sensitive to ethical diversity, and able to engage with colleagues and service users to create ways of working together that treat everyone fairly, take account of past injustices (including historical trauma), and present or repair moral injury. The idea of 'ethics work', developed by Sarah Banks, represents a valuable framework for thinking about what this involves on an everyday level.

Within the process of conducting research, ethics work entails building on, and being willing to go beyond, the kind of ethical contract and procedures that might be approved by an ethics committee or IRB. For instance, the process of informed consent that represents a core element of research ethics, reflects an assumption of individual autonomy. This is an important ethical perspective. However, from the perspective of relational ethics, it is possible to question whether individual autonomy around decision-making really captures what is happening. After all, a person completing a consent form is almost certainly thinking about what other people in their family or community might want them to do, and whether they trust the researcher who has asked them to be part of their project. From a process ethics perspective, the act of giving consent at one point in time does not really capture what is happening either – maybe two months into the study, the person will have a better understanding of what they are being asked to do, and may want to revisit their decision. From a participatory research perspective, a community group who are partners in a research study may take the view that consent should consider that what is good for the community, not just what is good for the individual research subject.

The example of a pluralistic perspective on ethical consent represents just one of many points in a research study where multiple ethical standpoints need to be taken into consideration. Ethics work comprises a set of skills and strategies that are required to be able to facilitate conversation and dialogue around such moments, including being able to handle emotions that may be evoked.

Although ethics work involves a capacity to flexibly adapt to a range of scenarios, it is also possible to identify some recurring themes. Possibly the most fundamental theme is around the experience of care. Giving and receiving care is a basic aspect of human relationships. No one can live or survive outside of the web of inter-dependence and mutual care. In that sense, the concept of a purely autonomous and self-contained individual is not consistent with the reality of human existence. Everyone functions in a relationship of care with other persons, as well as with the more-than-human world. A crucial aspect of that relationship is the experience of vulnerability.

A further major theme within ethics work is the experience of solidarity. To be able to provide effective care, and to receive sufficient care, there needs to be a willingness and capacity for people to stand together, and to stand up for each other. An important aspect of solidarity is acceptance of difference: differences between people around how they see things or go about doing things can be accommodated if there exists a sufficient degree of solidarity in terms of shared commitment to a common good.

A final theme concerns the nature of justice. A just world is one in which there is adequate care (and lack of carelessness) in how people relate to each other and the more-than-human world, and also strong traditions of mutual solidarity. Where we are now, a just world, defined in these terms, is not possible. As a consequence, in practical terms, a commitment to justice, means tackling *injustice* wherever it occurs.

The significance of justice, solidarity, and care permeate and motivate the entire body of work on participatory approaches to research. The capacity to engage in appropriate ethics work in relation to even the most micro-aspects of a study is a pre-requisite for effectively articulating these ethical dimensions. There exists a substantial literature on the ethics of care, and relational ethics, some of which is cited at relevant points in the present book, and further accessed through studies highlighted in the book. Valuable though that literature is, much of it is formulated from a standpoint of looking at broad areas of cultural and social life as a whole. By contrast, the focus of participatory research is close-up rather than wide-angle. The ethics of participatory research is concerned with what happens between people, in relationships, groups, and communities. It is therefore similar in focus to the ethics of therapy practice. The implication here is that ideas and skills around pluralistic ethics and ethics work may be of some value to therapy practitioners, supervisors, and trainers.

A pluralist approach to ethical issues in participatory research calls for consideration of different ethical perspectives associated with different cultural traditions. The discussion in the present book has emphasised the way of being associated with Indigenous cultural communities, as a model of egalitarian knowledge-building and decision-making based on a resolute ethic of care for other people as well as all aspects of the more-than-human world. While it is not possible to replicate Indigenous practices in research groups operating in advanced industrial societies, it is nevertheless feasible to learn from Indigenous knowledge and to support its continued existence, and hopefully its future flourishing.

Developing the practical relevance of participatory therapy research

The participatory counselling and psychotherapy studies highlighted in this book, and related participatory studies in cognate disciplines such as social work and health care, demonstrate the potential value of this methodological approach in relation to practical topics and questions in the therapy field. Participatory research has been applied to the investigation of many aspects of therapy. A wide range of participation-oriented research designs have been utilised. All of this is backed up by a massive, and expanding, literature on participatory research across the wider domain of health and social care, and the availability of a wealth of research guidelines and tools. In the context of a therapy research community in which most leading researchers espouse methodological diversity and pluralism, there are many opportunities for principles of participatory inquiry to be applied more widely, including in knowledge transfer (Granek and Nakash, 2016).

An implicit but unacknowledged dialogical and participatory approach is used in many therapy research studies. For example, many researchers carry out informal consultations with clients, service users, and therapy practitioners as a means of ensuring that their planned study is sufficiently aligned with the lived experience and priorities of these individuals. Such consultations are rarely described in dissertations, theses and published articles, for fear of being seen to engage in a research process that does not conform to whatever has been approved by their ethics committee or IRB. Most participatory make use of qualitative methods, such as interviews and focus groups. Within the qualitative studies research community, there has been a lot of attention devoted to the development of criteria and procedures for ensuring the trustworthiness and credibility (or validity) of qualitative studies. There is a broad acceptance that trustworthiness is enhanced by research analysis being audited by individuals outside of the main research team, by inviting informants (e.g., people interviewed in the study) to comment on the analysis, and other strategies that involve external perspectives being brought to bear on the research process (see McLeod, 2022 for further information on these procedures). An example of how trustworthiness procedures can be implemented can be found in a study by Garrison et al. (2023), who used multiple forms of external auditing and consultation. What they did was, in effect, very similar to what might happen in a participatory study, but without drawing on ideas from the participatory and co-production literature, such as giving participant voices more (or equal) weight.

At the present time, there are few participatory studies in any one area of therapy. Further studies are needed to be able to learn how participatory methods can contribute to cumulative knowledge production. Further studies are also necessary to evaluate the degree to which the findings of participatory research studies can make a difference to practice.

Ethics work in therapy practice

The concept of ethics work, with its origins in community-based participatory research, offers new ways of understanding ethical aspects of counselling and psychotherapy (Banks, 2016). Rather than viewing ethics as essentially concerned with contracting to keep clients safe, or regarding ethics as a value commitment to the uniqueness and other-ness of the client, the idea of ethics work transforms these facets into strands of practical action that sit alongside many other strands. The notion of ethics work reflects a pluralistic stance: it suggests that there is no single aspect of ethical awareness and attention that is definitive. Instead, doing what is right calls for attention to multiple elements of the practitioner-client relationship, and the development of multiple skills and competencies. Such an approach keeps the focus on what is happening on the ground in respect of specific contexts. A key skill in ethics work is to be able to identify multiple, ongoing ethics tasks within a case or organisation (Banks & Brydon-Miller, 2019).

An important area of ethics work, that is highly salient in participatory research but less salient in counselling and psychotherapy, centres on aligning practice with social justice. This task involves identifying relevant forms of injustice, making links with other groups that are also working to overcome that source of injustice, developing a narrative that allows individuals to make sense of how their own struggles are part of a bigger picture, and finding tangible ways of making a difference. Another strand of ethics work that is central in participatory research is being open to learning from people who have knowledge from experience rather than knowledge acquired through professional training and study. Ethics work also calls for a capacity to use moral imagination to anticipate and prevent moral injury arising from co-researchers feeling betrayed by tokenistic consultation and shared decision-making that does not take their views seriously. Being able to consciously identify these – and other – forms of ethics work makes it possible for therapists to begin to appreciate how all aspects of therapy depend not only on technical competence (i.e., therapy skills) and self-awareness, but also on their ability to engage constructively with the moral and ethical significance of what therapy interactions.

These ideas support and extend what might be described as the increasing ethicisation of therapy. A growing number of therapy writers and researchers have developed perspectives for thinking about the many different types of moral injury that are presented by therapy clients, and the notion that therapy can be a force for social justice. Some therapists believe that spending time in sessions exploring ethical issues with a client, such as the meaning of informed consent, can lead to more effective therapy because it helps the client to make a more whole-hearted commitment to the process of change (Trachsel & grosse Holtforth, 2019).

Affirming and cultivating the client's dialogical resources

A key assumption in participatory research is that practical knowledge arises from a dialectical process based on dialogue between people who speak from different life experiences and perspectives (Johnson, 2017). This approach invites reflection on the question: what makes it possible for a person to convey their relevant life experience, position on a topic, within such conversations? One of the most striking features of participatory research is that many of the most successful projects are based on situations where service user (and other) co-researchers are drawn from a community, or are part of an ongoing inquiry group, rather than being disparate individuals who offer their views on an essentially solo basis. In relation to this question, Faulkner (2017) suggests that, to be able to convey experiential knowledge in an effective and coherent manner, the person needs to be able to build up their understanding and narrative repertoire within a supportive group of like-minded individuals. In the field of participatory research, this occurs in co-researchers who are drawn from Indigenous communities, or are members of pre-existing organisations such as domestic violence services. Faulkner (2017) argued that effective participatory research in mental health was only possible when the survivor research and Mad Studies movements reached a stage of being able to offer clients and service users opportunities to join mutual support groups. More recently, the flourishing of participatory research in neurodiversity required the establishment of meetings and conversations that allowed people in that community to work out what they wanted to say, and how they wanted to say it.

At the present time, routine counselling and psychotherapy practice does not operate like that at all. Before seeing a therapist, few prospective clients have had opportunities to talk about what it means for them to feel anxious or depressed (or whatever their problem might be) or to share ideas about what they might want from therapy. The consequence is that, on entering therapy, they are not in a position to readily articulate their therapy preferences. On the whole, therapists rarely ask about the client's preferences, or expect a client to have much to say on this topic, despite the evidence that preference accommodation can enhance therapy outcome (Norcross & Cooper, 2021). It could be valuable for future research to explore the possibility that opportunities to share personal experiences of adversity in a peer group might enable a person to make more effective use of therapy. A version of this strategy was a key element of the social action approach to therapy (Hoggett et al, 2022; Holland, 1992; Melluish & Bulmer, 1999).

Co-design of therapy services

Participatory research is often undertaken in order to improve the quality of services. A good example of this is the programme of participatory research that leads to the publication of a set of guidelines for therapy assessment for trauma survivors (Sweeney, 2021). These guidelines are available to any practitioners and therapy clinics, to assist them in enhancing their procedures for client assessment. A more direct way of using a participatory approach is for practitioners and managers in a service to work with service users and others to produce a plan of action for improving that specific service. This approach has been described as co-design or co-production of services. When it includes a phase of analysing the outcomes of the changes that have been introduced, it is sometimes described as participatory action research. There is a lot of overlap between these models. In addition, some projects described as participatory research studies may incorporate an action or implementation phase.

The skill-set, and underlying philosophical assumptions associated with participatory research, are similar to those required for co-design and co-production. Involvement in participatory research (e.g., in the context of an academic degree programme) can therefore be viewed as good preparation for undertaking service co-design at a later stage in one's career.

The use of co-design is increasing in significance within the field of counselling and psychotherapy. One reason for this is the growing use of information technology in the form of apps, virtual reality simulations, avatars, and online therapy: co-design using consumers to try out new devices has always been a central aspect of product development in the IT sector. A further reason is that it is clear that there exist many sub-groups of clients who are not well-served by existing services, and need therapy to be configured in a different way to make it accessible and relevant for them. An example of this is the increasing recognition of the need to adapt standard counselling and psychotherapy when working with women who are experiencing perinatal mental health issues (Millett et al., 2018).

The value of co-design of counselling, psychotherapy and mental health services has been demonstrated in a range of settings, such as a health service therapy clinic (Cooper et al., 2016), counselling for people with learning disabilities who have been raped (Olsen & Carter, 2016), and development of therapeutic activities to support individuals with long-term mental health difficulties (Illarregi, 2021; Illarregi et al., 2023).

Greater use of co-design by counselling and psychotherapy clinics and services has the potential to enhance the accessibility and helpfulness of therapy for local communities. An important step forward would be to integrate co-design into an ongoing quality improvement programme over an extended period of time, making use of the kind of routine outcome monitoring data that many therapy services are already collecting. Such a process would not only make it possible for a service to align its offering with what clients need, but would also be beneficial for those former clients who were involved in the co-design team (Mayer & McKenzie, 2017).

Principles of co-design are also relevant in relation to how therapists and clients work together in routine practice. Pluralistic therapy is an explicitly co-design approach, in which the therapist facilitates a process of shared decision-making through which both client and therapist ideas about therapy tasks and activities shape what happens in sessions (McLeod, 2018; McLeod & Sundet, 2022). Other examples of co-designed therapy can be found in case reports by Hartogs et al. (2012) and Robbins et al. (2008).

Co-design in therapy training

Given the potential relevance of participatory research skills and strategies for therapy practice, it may be helpful to enable counselling and psychotherapy students and trainees to gain first-hand experience of this approach within training programmes. Students may benefit from being co-participants in research projects. It may also be useful to enable students to co-design sections of the training syllabus, or specific events and workshops within it.

Extending the reach of an ethics of care

Participatory research is increasingly viewed as an approach to knowledge production that can make a vital contribution to both humanising health and social care, and making services more efficient in terms of cost-effective use of scarce resources.

Within the research community that has used participatory research in studies of mental health and recovery, there has been frustration that such studies have mainly been aimed at generating relatively limited improvements to existing services, rather than asking fundamental questions about whether these services should exist at all, or how they might be radically re-imagined.

An example of this sense of disappointment can be found in an important paper by Rose and Kalathil (2019) who argues that the initial promise of participatory research and co-design, around democratising decision-making and giving service users and the public a meaningful say in what happens, is untenable and unrealistic. The essential limitation of participatory inquiry, for Rose and Kalathil (2019), is that it is grounded in a Eurocentric worldview that privileges a rational, technical-scientific way of knowing that operates to defend the interests of those in power. They point out that participatory projects do not take place in a neutral 'third space' between the world of those with power, and those without. Instead, studies almost always operate within institutions and cognitive frameworks that are controlled by the established professions. While the existence of collegial, friendly, and caring relationships between co-researcher members of a participatory inquiry team and a sense of solidarity around addressing injustice are undoubtedly valuable achievements, they only go so far; beyond that, there remain deep-rooted differences in perspective.

A striking example of this kind of tension can be found in the area of research on psychotherapeutic interventions for people in American Indian and Alaska Native communities. This work has been supported by several decades of collaborative, participatory, and Indigenous-controlled programmes of research (Gone, 2022). Despite the degree to which Indigenous communities have been able to control the research agenda, a recent review of recommended therapies for clients within this cultural group placed evidence-based mainstream therapies first in the list, with grassroots Indigenous approaches and traditional healing being placed last (Wendt et al., 2022).

The limitations of contemporary participatory research in counselling, psychotherapy and related fields, are highlighted by reflecting on what has been achieved, and what is missing from the literature it has generated over the past 30 years. It could be argued that two very big areas are missing, or at best minimally represented. One of these is the issue of climate, pollution, biodiversity loss, and the whole troubled relationship between human civilisation and the more-than-human world. The second area relates to the multiple issues associated with racism, colonialism, and White privilege. Although there is plenty being written about how therapy might play a part in addressing climate change and racism, almost all of it reflects a professional voice (e.g., Morgan et al., 2022), or at best a client voice filtered through academic theoretical and methodological lenses (e.g., Budziszewska & Jonsson, 2022). It is very hard to identify examples of therapy studies or action/change projects around climate change and racism, where those directly affected by the issue are able to shape the research process by being in a co-researcher role or have control of that process.

It might be possible for participatory research in counselling and psychotherapy to make a more decisive contribution to overcoming the powerful forces of institutional control and resistance to change highlighted by Rose and Kalathil (2019), while at the same time creating more of a space for participatory research into big issues such as climate change and racism, by employing the kinds of ethical perspectives discussed in the present book as a framework for therapy practice.

Therapy can be viewed as a way of extending the reach of an ethics of care into areas of social life in which it has lost traction. The most significant programmes of participatory research in therapy, such as the work of Lisa Goodman and colleagues with marginalised and depressed women, and that of Angela Sweeney and colleagues around the entry point of survivors of trauma and betrayal into therapy (i.e., assessment), can be understood as representing sustained practical initiatives for bringing an ethics of care into the approach taken by therapists and the institutions in which they work. By investigating these topics in a participatory manner, with clients and service users centrally involved in the knowledge-creating process, it becomes possible to see that therapist theories and skills are not the biggest part of what is going wrong. Instead, when the knowledge by experience of clients and service users (and frontline practitioners) is harnessed, it becomes evident that the bigger part of what is going wrong is an absence of solidarity, justice, and care.

A smaller-scale example of what can become visible when a participatory approach is used can be seen in the findings of the study by Matheson and Weightman (2021a), in which patients who had received psychotherapy for complex post-traumatic stress disorder interviewed each other and took the lead in analysing the interview data. The principal researcher in this project was a therapist and Doctoral student who aimed to give participants as much space and support as possible to develop their own ideas. What emerged from this study had little resemblance to the trauma theories and interventions used by the therapists who had treated these patients. Rather, what they talked about in the interviews was the central importance of relationships: solidarity, mutual support, trust, and care. And also the requirement that there should be sufficient time to allow these qualities to flourish. From a pluralistic ethics perspective, Matheson and Weightman (2021a, 2021b) can be understood to have investigated the very big question of how people get their lives back following exposure to intense experiences of betrayal and cruelty: events that utterly shattered their belief in a just and caring world.

Conclusions

The key take-home messages from this book are that participatory research in the area of counselling and psychotherapy has the potential to generate new insights and support innovative forms of practice, and that to do participatory research well requires attention to moral and ethical issues beyond (but also including) the kinds of issues addressed in contractual ethical codes. Integrating opportunities to engage in participatory research and co-design into therapist training, would enable students and trainees to learn about doing ethics work that calls out injustice, and supports solidarity and care. These areas of learning are likely to lead to being a better therapist and to be in a position to work alongside other professions and community groups that espouse similar values.

Topics for reflection and discussion

1 What has been your experience of solidarity in your own life? How might that personal experience inform your work as a therapist or researcher?
2 Using a therapy transcript, recording, or video, or your recall of a recent therapy session, reflect on the possible moral and ethical significance of what the client says, and how the therapist responds. As well as ethical and moral meanings specific to that particular therapy case, pay attention to how the conversation refers to the importance of care and solidarity in the life of the client and the client-therapy relationship, and to implicit or explicit references to justice and an image of what a 'good life' might look like.
3 The ethical, kinship-based worldview associated with Indigenous cultures and communities, has the potential to provide therapy researchers and practitioners with a distinctive perspective that has the potential to support a social justice standpoint. Where do you position yourself in relation to that perspective? In your view, what are the advantages and disadvantages of following that path?
4 As a therapist, which elements of co-design do you already incorporate into your work with clients? What might be the advantages and disadvantages of adopting a more fully co-design or co-production approach?
5 As a client in therapy, to what extent, in what ways, does your therapist (or various therapists you may have seen) encourage you to contribute your own ideas about how therapy might be most helpful for you, in the spirit of co-design or co-production? How valuable has this aspect of therapy been for you (or how valuable might it be, if it was given more emphasis)?
6 Do you agree that participatory therapy research has not sufficiently engaged with major societal challenges around the climate crisis and colonialism? What kinds of participatory research projects could you imagine that might advance this agenda?
7 What is your response to the idea that therapy – both as a form of practice within contemporary society, and as an activity that supports individuals and families to build better lives – fundamentally involves a process of extending the reach of an ethics of care?
8 If you were a trainer or lecturer on a counselling or psychotherapy training programme, how might you introduce a co-design or participatory research activity into the curriculum? What would you expect, or hope, that trainees might gain from such an activity?

References

Adams, L. B., Baxter, S. L., Lightfoot, A. F., Gottfredson, N., Golin, C., Jackson, L. C., ... & Powell, W. (2021). Refining Black men's depression measurement using participatory approaches: A concept mapping study. *BMC Public Health, 21*(1), 1–10.

Aggleton, P., Broom, A., & Moss, J. (Eds.) (2019). *Practical justice: Principles, practice and social change.* Routledge.

Ammentorp, J., Wolderslund, M., Timmermann, C., Larsen, H., Steffensen, K. D., Nielsen, A., ... & Gulbrandsen, P. (2018). How participatory action research changed our view of the challenges of shared decision-making training. *Patient Education and Counseling, 101*(4), 639–646.

Anae, M. (2019). Pacific research methodologies and relational ethics. *Oxford Research Encyclopedia of Education.* https://doi.org/10.1093/acrefore/9780190264093.013.529

Anjum, R. L., Copeland, S., & Rocca, E. (Eds.) (2020). *Rethinking causality, complexity and evidence for the unique patient. A CauseHealth resource for health professionals and the clinical encounter.* Springer.

Arizaga, J. A., Polo, A. J., & Martinez-Torteya, C. (2020). Heterogeneous trajectories of depression symptoms in Latino youth. *Journal of Clinical Child & Adolescent Psychology, 49*(1), 94–105.

Asfeldt, M., & Beames, S. (2017). Trusting the journey: Embracing the unpredictable and difficult to measure nature of wilderness educational expeditions. *Journal of Experiential Education, 40*(1), 72–86.

Bacha, K., Hanley, T., & Winter, L. A. (2020). 'Like a human being, I was an equal, I wasn't just a patient': Service users' perspectives on their experiences of relationships with staff in mental health services. *Psychology and Psychotherapy: Theory, Research and Practice, 93*(2), 367–386.

Banks, S. (2016). Everyday ethics in professional life: Social work as ethics work. *Ethics and Social Welfare, 10*(1), 35–52.

Banks, S., & Brydon-Miller, M. (2019). *Ethics in participatory research for health and social well-being: Cases and commentaries.* Routledge.

Baranowski, K., Bhattacharyya, S., Herbst, B. R., Ameen, E. J., Cote, L. M., Gonzalez, C. C., Gonzalez, D., Jones, S., Reynolds, J. D., Goodman, L. A., & Miville, M. L. (2017). Community and public arena advocacy training challenges, supports, and recommendations in counseling psychology: A participatory qualitative inquiry. *Journal for Social Action in Counseling and Psychology, 8*(2), 70–97.

Barbic, S., Brooks, E., Lassak, N., Khaleghi, M., Zenone, M., Ow, N., ... & Mathias, S. (2022). "It cannot be boring!": Developing a measure of function for young adults accessing integrated youth services. *Journal of Patient-Reported Outcomes*, *6*(1), 1–14.

Barbuto, R., Biggeri, M., & Griffo, G. (2011). Life project, peer counselling and self-help groups as tools to expand capabilities, agency and human rights. *Alter*, *5*(3), 192–205.

Barkham, M. (2014). Practice-based research networks: Origins, overview, obstacles, and opportunities. *Counselling and Psychotherapy Research, 14(3)*, 167–173.

Barnes, H. M., Gunn, T. R., Barnes, A. M., Muriwai, E., Wetherell, M., & McCreanor, T. (2017). Feeling and spirit: Developing an indigenous wairua approach to research. *Qualitative Research*, *17*(3), 313–325.

Bartholomew, T. T., Pérez-Rojas, A. E., Lockard, A. J., & Locke, B. D. (2017). "Research doesn't fit in a 50-minute hour": The phenomenology of therapists' involvement in research at a university counseling center. *Counselling Psychology Quarterly*, *30*(3), 255–273.

Baumann, S. E., Kameg, B. N., Wiltrout, C. T., Murdoch, D., Pelcher, L., & Burke, J. G. (2024). Visualizing mental health through the lens of Pittsburgh youth: A collaborative filmmaking study during COVID-19. *Health Promotion Practice*, *25*(3), 368–382.

Baumann, S. E., Lhaki, P., & Burke, J. G. (2020). Collaborative filmmaking: A participatory, visual research method. *Qualitative Health Research*, *30*(14), 2248–2264.

Bear, R., Choate, P. W., & Lindstrom, G. (2022). Reconsidering Maslow and the hierarchy of needs from a First Nations' perspective. *Aotearoa New Zealand Social Work Review*, *34*(2), 30–41.

Beck, B., Halling, S., McNabb, M., Miller, D., Rowe, J. O., & Schulz, J. (2005). On navigating despair: Reports from psycho-therapists. *Journal of Religion and Health*, *44*(2), 187–205.

Beeker, T., Glück, R. K., Ziegenhagen, J., Göppert, L., Jänchen, P., Krispin, H., ... & von Peter, S. (2021). Designed to clash? Reflecting on the practical, personal, and structural challenges of collaborative research in psychiatry. *Frontiers in Psychiatry*, *12*, 701312.

Beetham, T., Gabriel, L., & James, H. (2019). Young children's narrations of relational recovery: A school-based group for children who have experienced domestic violence. *Journal of Family Violence*, *34*(6), 565–575.

Bemak, F., & Chung, R. C.-Y. (2021). A culturally responsive intervention for modern-day refugees: A multiphase model of psychotherapy, social justice, and human rights. In J. D. Aten & J. Hwang (Eds.), *Refugee mental health* (pp. 103–136). American Psychological Association.

Bennett, V., Gill, C., Miller, P., Lewis, P., Ypag, N., Hamilton-Giachritsis, C., & Lavi, I. (2022). Developing a novel co-produced methodology to understand 'real-world' help-seeking in online peer–peer communities by young people experiencing emotional abuse and neglect. *Health Expectations*, *25*(6), 3124–3142.

Birrell, P. J., & Freyd, J. J. (2006). Betrayal trauma: Relational models of harm and healing. *Journal of Trauma Practice*, *5*(1), 49–63.

Blair, C., Best, P., Burns, P., Campbell, A., Davidson, G., Duffy, J., ... & Yap, J. (2022). "Getting involved in research": A co-created, co-delivered and co-analysed course for those with lived experience of health and social care services. *Research Involvement and Engagement*, *8*(1), 1–16.

Blakley, L. (2022). Learning to become a more ethically focused practitioner researcher: Developing through the research ethics process. *Ethics and Social Welfare*, *16*(3), 322–331.

Blunden, N. (2020). "And we are a human being". Coproduced reflections on person-centred psychotherapy in plural and dissociative identity. *Psychotherapy and Politics International*, e1578, https://doi.org/10.1002/ppi.1578.

Boydell, K. M., Ball, J., Curtis, J., De Jager, A., Kalucy, M., Lappin, J., ... & Watkins, A. (2018). A novel landscape for understanding physical and mental health: Body mapping research with youth experiencing psychosis. *Art/Research International: A Transdisciplinary Journal, 3*(2), 236–261.

Bradbury, H. (Ed.) (2015). *SAGE handbook of action research: Participative inquiry and practice*. SAGE.

Brownlie, J. (2014). *Ordinary relationships: A sociological study of emotions, reflexivity and culture*. Palgrave Macmillan.

Brownlie, J., &Anderson, S. (2017). Thinking sociologically about kindness: Puncturing the blasé in the ordinary city. *Sociology, 51*, 1222–1238.

Brubacher, L. J., Dewey, C. E., Tatty, N., Healey Akearok, G. K., Cunsolo, A., Humphries, S., & Harper, S. L. (2021). "Sewing is part of our tradition": A case study of sewing as a strategy for arts-based inquiry in health research with Inuit women. *Qualitative Health Research, 31*(14), 2602–2616.

Bryan, C. J., Tipton, E., & Yeager, D. S. (2021). Behavioural science is unlikely to change the world without a heterogeneity revolution. *Nature Human Behaviour, 5*(8), 980–989.

Bryant-Davis, T. (2019). The cultural context of trauma recovery: Considering the posttraumatic stress disorder practice guideline and intersectionality. *Psychotherapy, 56*(3), 400–408.

Brydon-Miller, M., & Hilsen, A. I. (2016). Where rivers meet: Exploring the confluence of ecofeminism, covenantal ethics, and action research. In M. Phillips & N. Rumens (Eds.), *Contemporary perspectives on ecofeminism* (pp. 95–108). Routledge.

Budziszewska, M., & Jonsson, S. E. (2022). Talking about climate change and eco-anxiety in psychotherapy: A qualitative analysis of patients' experiences. *Psychotherapy, 59*(4), 606–615.

Camargo Plazas, P., Cameron, B. L., Milford, K., Hunt, L. R., Bourque-Bearskin, L., & Santos Salas, A. (2019). Engaging Indigenous youth through popular theatre: Knowledge mobilization of Indigenous peoples' perspectives on access to healthcare services. *Action Research, 17*(4), 492–509.

Carlton, J., Peasgood, T., Khan, S., Barber, R., Bostock, J., & Keetharuth, A. D. (2020). An emerging framework for fully incorporating public involvement (PI) into patient-reported outcome measures (PROMs). *Journal of Patient-Reported Outcomes, 4*(1), 1–10.

Carroll, M., & Shaw, E. (2013). *Ethical maturity in the helping professions: Making difficult life and work decisions.* Jessica Kingsley.

Caslin, M., Georgiou, H., Davies, C., & Spoor, S. (2022). No laughing matter: Exploring the role of comedy when researching employment barriers with disabled young people. In S. Frankel (Ed.). *Establishing child centred practice in a changing world* (pp. 47–60). Emerald Publishing Limited.

Castonguay, L. G., Barkham, M., Youn, S. J., & Page, A. C. (2021). Practice-based evidence—Findings from routine clinical settings. In M. Barkham, W. Lutz, & L. G. Castonguay (Eds.), *Bergin and Garfield's handbook of psychotherapy and behavior change:* 50th anniversary edition (pp. 191–222). Wiley.

Castonguay, L. G., Nelson, D. L., Boutselis, M. A., Chiswick, N. R., Damer, D. D., Hemmelstein, N. A., ... & Borkovec, T. D. (2010). Psychotherapists, researchers, or both? A qualitative analysis of psychotherapists' experiences in a practice research network. *Psychotherapy: Theory, research, practice, training, 47*(3), 345.

Cedar, L., Coleman, A., Haythorne, D., Jones, P., Mercieca, D., & Ramsden, E. (2022). Child agency and therapy in primary school. *Education 3-13, 50*(4), 452–470.

Centre for Social Justice and Community Action (2012). *Community-based participatory research: A guide to ethical principles and practice*. https://www.publicengagement.ac.uk/

sites/default/files/2023-08/cbpr_ethics_guide_web_november_2012.pdf (retrieved 18th November 2024).

Chandanabhumma, P. P., Fàbregues, S., Oetzel, J., Duran, B., & Ford, C. (2023). Examining the influence of group diversity on the functioning of community-based participatory research partnerships: A mixed methods study. *American Journal of Community Psychology, 71*(1–2), 242–254.

Chapman, S., & Schwartz, J. P. (2012). Rejecting the null: Research and social justice means asking different questions. *Counseling and Values, 57*(1), 24–30.

Charura, D., & Clyburn, S. (2023). Critical race theory: A methodology for research in psychotherapy. In K. Tudor & J. Wyatt (Eds.), *Qualitative Research approaches for psychotherapy* (pp. 72–86). Routledge.

Chevalier, J. M., & Buckles, D. J. (2019). *Participatory action research: Theory and methods for engaged inquiry*. Routledge.

Chubb, L. A., Fouché, C. B., & Sadeh Kengah, K. (2022). Baraza as method: Adapting a traditional conversational space for data collection and pathways for change. *Qualitative Social Work, 21*(5), 914–931.

Connell, J., Carlton, J., Grundy, A., Taylor Buck, E., Keetharuth, A. D., Ricketts, T., ... & Brazier, J. (2018). The importance of content and face validity in instrument development: Lessons learnt from service users when developing the Recovering Quality of Life measure (ReQoL). *Quality of Life Research, 27*(7), 1893–1902.

Conrad, D. (2020). Youth participatory action research and applied theatre engagement: Supporting Indigenous Youth survivance and resurgence. *Theatre Research in Canada, 41*(2), 258–277.

Conrad, D. (2023). Engagement, authenticity, and advocacy in "Youth Uncensored": Ethics in applied theater research with street-involved youth. *Qualitative Inquiry, 29*(2), 365–373.

Cook, T., Brandon, T., Zonouzi, M., & Thomson, L. (2019). Destabilizing equilibriums: Harnessing the power of disruption in participatory action research. *Educational Action Research, 27*(3), 379–395.

Cooper, K., Gillmore, C., & Hogg, L. (2016). Experience-based co-design in an adult psychological therapies service. *Journal of Mental Health, 25*(1), 36–40.

Cornwall, A., & Jewkes, R. (1995). What is participatory research? *Social Science and Medicine, 41*, 1667–1676.

Costa, L., Voronka, J., Landry, D., Reid, J., Mcfarlane, B., Reville, D., & Church, K. (2012). "Recovering our stories": A small act of resistance. *Studies in Social Justice, 6*(1), 85–101.

Country, B., Suchet-Pearson, S., Wright, S., Lloyd, K., Tofa, M., Burarrwanga, L., ... & Maymuru, D. (2020). Bunbum ga dhä-yu t agum: To make it right again, to remake. *Social & Cultural Geography, 21*(7), 985–1001.

Country, N., Duncan, M., Duncan, R., & Tait, L. (2022). Traiyimbat olkainbala wei ov dum tings| trying out all kinds of ways of doing things: Co-creative multisensory methods in collaborative research. *Social & Cultural Geography, 23*(8), 1097–1117.

Courcy, I., & Koniou, I. (2024). A scoping review of the use of photo-elicitation and photovoice with autistic and neurodiverse people. Moving towards more inclusive research? *Disability & Society, 39*(5), 1317–1338.

Crawford, M. J., Robotham, D., Thana, L., Patterson, S., Weaver, T., Barber, R., ... & Rose, D. (2011). Selecting outcome measures in mental health: The views of service users. *Journal of Mental Health, 20*(4), 336–346.

Creadick, A. (2010). *Perfectly average: The pursuit of normality in Postwar America*. University of Massachusetts Press.

Danchev, D., & Ross, A. (2014). *Research ethics for counsellors, nurses and social workers.* Sage.

Davies, A., & Morris, M. (2018). *A collaborative inquiry into the positioning of gender practice within systemic psychotherapy.* SAGE Research Methods Cases in Psychology. https://dx.doi.org/10.4135/9781526440952

Dawson, L., Hay, J., & Rosling, N. (2021). Therapeutic creativity and the lived experience of grief in the collaborative fiction film. *Lost Property. Research for All, 5*(2), 227–245.

De Jager, A., Tewson, A., Ludlow, B., & Boydell, K. (2016). Embodied ways of storying the self: A systematic review of body-mapping. *Forum Qualitative Sozialforschung/forum: Qualitative Social Research, 17*(2). http://openresearch.ocadu.ca/id/eprint/1206/

de Ossorno Garcia, S., Salhi, L., Sefi, A., & Hanley, T. (2021). The Session Wants and Need Outcome Measure (SWAN-OM): The development of a brief outcome measure for single-sessions of web-based support. *Frontiers in Psychology*, 4900. https://doi.org/10.3389/fpsyg.2021.748145

Deloria, V. Jr. (2012). *C.G. Jung and the Sioux tradition. Dreams, visions, nature, and the primitive.* Spring Journal Books.

Demers, J. M., Gregus, S., & Petts, R. A. (2022). New communities, new relationships: Reflections from junior faculty engaging in community-based research. *Journal of Interpersonal Violence, 37*, 17.

Denborough, D. (2011). Collective narrative practice: Eliciting and richly describing local skills and knowledges in communities responding to hardship. PhD Thesis, La Trobe University.

Denborough, D. (2012). A storyline of collective narrative practice: A history of ideas, social projects and partnerships. *International Journal of Narrative Therapy & Community Work*, 1, 40–65. https://dulwichcentre.com.au/wp-content/uploads/2020/12/A_storyline_of_collective_narrative_practice_a_history_of_ideas_social_projects_and_partnerships_by_David_Denborough-1.pdf (retrieved 13th February 2023).

Denborough, D., Koolmatrie, C., Mununggirritj, D., Marika, D., Dhurrkay, W., & Yunupingu, M. (2006). Linking stories and initiatives: A narrative approach to working with the skills and knowledge of communities. *International Journal of Narrative Therapy & Community Work, 2006*(2), 19–51. https://dulwichcentre.com.au/linking-stories-and-initiatives.pdf (retrieved 13th February 2023).

Denner, J., Bean, S., Campe, S., Martinez, J., & Torres, D. (2019). Negotiating trust, power, and culture in a research–practice partnership. *AERA Open, 5*(2), 2332858419858635.

Desai, M. U., Bellamy, C., Guy, K., Costa, M., O'Connell, M. J., & Davidson, L. (2019). "If You Want to Know About the Book, Ask the Author": Enhancing community engagement through participatory research in clinical mental health settings. *Behavioral Medicine, 45*(2), 177–187.

DiAngelo, R. (2019). *White fragility: Why it's so hard for white people to talk about racism.* Penguin.

Dirik, A., Barrett, K., Bennison, G., Collinson, S., & Sandhu, S. (2018). A conceptual review of family involvement in acute mental health treatment: Methodology and personal reflections. *Research for All, 2*(2), 257–266.

Doroud, N., Fossey, E., Fortune, T., Brophy, L., & Mountford, L. (2022). A journey of living well: A participatory photovoice study exploring recovery and everyday activities with people experiencing mental illness. *Journal of Mental Health, 31*(2), 246–254.

Doucet, A. (2008). "From her side of the gossamer wall(s)": Reflexivity and relational knowing. *Qualitative Sociology, 31*(1), 73–87.

Dreyer, M., Kosow, H., Bauer, A., Chonkova, B., Kozarev, V., & Timotijevic, L. (2021). Public engagement with research: Citizens' views on motivations, barriers and support. *Research for All, 5*(2), 302–319.

Dutta, U., Azad, A. K., & Hussain, S. M. (2022). Counterstorytelling as epistemic justice: Decolonial community-based praxis from the global south. *American Journal of Community Psychology*, *69*(1–2), 59–70.

Dwyer, P., Acevedo, S. M., Brown, H. M., Grapel, J., Jones, S. C., Nachman, B. R., ... & Williams, Z. J. (2021). An expert roundtable discussion on experiences of autistic autism researchers. *Autism in Adulthood*, *3*(3), 209–220.

Ejbye-Ernst, D., & Jorring, N. T. (2017). Doing it collaboratively! Addressing the dilemmas of designing quantitative effect studies on narrative family therapy in a local clinical context. *Journal of Systemic Therapies*, *36*(1), 48–66.

Engage for Equity Research Team. (2017). *Promising practices of CBPR and community engaged research partnerships*. University of New Mexico, Albuquerque. https://engageforequity.org/wp-content/uploads/2017/12/Promising-Practices-Guide-12.7.12.pdf

Erikainen, S., Stewart, E., Chan, S., Cunningham-Burley, S., Ilson, S., King, G., Porteous, C., & Sinclair, S. (2021). Towards a feminist philosophy of engagements in health-related research. *Wellcome Open Research*, *6*, 58.

Etherington, K. (2000). *Narrative approaches to working with adult male survivors of child sexual abuse: The clients', the counsellor's and the researcher's story*. Jessica Kingsley.

Etherington, K. (2002). Working together: Editing a book as narrative research methodology. *Counselling and Psychotheraphy Research*, *2*(3), 167–176.

Etherington, K. (2003). *Trauma, the body and transformation: A narrative inquiry*. Jessica Kingsley Publishers.

Etherington, K. (2007). Ethical research in reflexive relationships. *Qualitative Inquiry*, *13*(5), 599–616.

Etherington, K. (2009). Ethical research in reflexive relationships. In L. Gabriel & R. Casemore (Eds.), *Relational ethics in practice: Narratives from counselling and psychotherapy* (pp. 58–75). Brunner-Routledge.

Evans, J., Rose, D., Flach, C., Csipke, E., Glossop, H., Mccrone, P., ... & Wykes, T. (2012). VOICE: Developing a new measure of service users' perceptions of inpatient care, using a participatory methodology. *Journal of Mental Health*, *21*(1), 57–71.

Faulkner, A. (2004). *The ethics of survivor research: Guidelines for the ethical conduct of research carried out by mental health service users and survivors*. Policy Press.

Faulkner, A. (2017). Survivor research and Mad Studies: The role and value of experiential knowledge in mental health research. *Disability & Society*, *32*(4), 500–520.

Faulkner, A., Kelly, K., Gibson, S., Gillard, S., Samuels, L., & Sweeney, A. (2023). Respect for the journey: A survivor-led investigation of undergoing psychotherapy assessment. *Social Psychiatry and Psychiatric Epidemiology*, *53*, 1803–1811.

Ferrazzi, P., Tagalik, S., Christie, P., Karetak, J., Baker, K., & Angalik, L. (2019). Aajiiqatigiingniq: An inuit consensus methodology in qualitative health research. *International Journal of Qualitative Methods*, *18*, 1–9.

Fine, M. (2006). Bearing witness: Methods for researching oppression and resistance—A textbook for critical research. *Social Justice Research*, *19*(1), 83–108.

Fine, M. (2013). Echoes of Bedford: A 20-year social psychology memoir on participatory action research hatched behind bars. *American Psychologist*, *68*(8), 687–698.

Fine, M. (2016). Just methods in revolting times. *Qualitative Research in Psychology*, *13*(4), 347–365.

Fine, M. (2017). *Just research in contentious times: Widening the methodological imagination*. Teachers College Press.

Fine, M., & Torre, M. E. (2019). Critical participatory action research: A feminist project for validity and solidarity. *Psychology of Women Quarterly*, *43*(4), 433–444.

Finfgeld, D. L. (1999). Courage as a process of pushing beyond the struggle. *Qualitative Health Research*, *9*(6), 803–814.

Finlay, L. (2020). Ethical research? Examining knotty, moment-to-moment challenges throughout the research process. In S. Bager-Charleson & A. McBeath (Eds.), *Enjoying Research in Counselling and Psychotherapy Qualitative, Quantitative and Mixed Methods Research* (pp. 115–135). Palgrave Macmillan.

Fiske, A. (2019). *Kama Muta: Discovering the connecting emotion*. Routledge.

Frank, J. D. (1974). Psychotherapy: The restoration of morale. *American Journal of Psychiatry*, *131*, 271–274.

Fricker, M. (2007). *Epistemic injustice: Power and the ethics of knowing*. Oxford University Press.

Fricker, M. (2017). Evolving concepts of epistemic injustice. In I. J. Kidd, J. Medina, & G. Pohlhaus Jr (Eds.), *Routledge handbook of epistemic injustice* (pp. 53–60). Routledge.

Gabriel, L. (2009). Exploring the researcher-contributor research alliance. In L. Gabriel & R. Casemore (Eds.), *Relational ethics in practice: Narratives from counselling and psychotherapy* (pp. 147–157). Brunner-Routledge.

Gabriel, L., & Casemore, R. (Eds.) (2009). *Relational ethics in practice: Narratives from counselling and psychotherapy*. Routledge.

Gabriel, L., James, H., Cronin-Davis, J., Tizro, Z., Beetham, T., Hullock, A., & Raynar, A. (2017). Reflexive research with mothers and children victims of domestic violence. *Counselling and Psychotherapy Research*, *17*(2), 157–165.

Gabriel, L., Tizro, Z., James, H., Cronin-Davis, J., Beetham, T., Corbally, A., ... & Hill, S. (2018). "Give me some space": Exploring youth to parent aggression and violence. *Journal of Family Violence*, *33*(2), 161–169.

Gaddis, S. (2004). Re-positioning traditional research: Centring clients' accounts in the construction of professional therapy knowledges. *International Journal of Narrative Therapy & Community Work*, *4*(2), 1–12.

Garrison, Y. L., Jiao, T., Vaz, S., Shah, S., Reeves, D., Murphy, S., Lin, C.-L. R., & Pak, S. (2023). A qualitative study of women of color group psychotherapists: The wellspring of collective healing. *Journal of Counseling Psychology*, *70*(1), 1–15.

Gibson, K., & Cartwright, C. (2014). Young clients' narratives of the purpose and outcome of counselling. *British Journal of Guidance & Counselling*, *42*(5), 511–524.

Goldsmith, L. P., Morshead, R., McWilliam, C., Forbes, G., Ussher, M., Simpson, A., ... & Gillard, S. (2019). Co-producing randomized controlled trials: How do we work together? *Frontiers in Sociology*, 21. https://doi.org/10.3389/fsoc.2019.00021

Gone, J. P. (2017). "It felt like violence": Indigenous knowledge traditions and the postcolonial ethics of academic inquiry and community engagement. *American Journal of Community Psychology*, *60*(3–4), 353–360.

Gone, J. P. (2019). Considering Indigenous research methodologies: Critical reflections by an Indigenous knower. *Qualitative Inquiry*, *25*(1), 45–56.

Gone, J. P. (2022). Researching with American Indian and Alaska Native communities: Pursuing partnerships for psychological inquiry in service to Indigenous futurity. In H. Cooper, M. N. Coutanche, L. M. McMullen, A. T. Panter, D. Rindskopf, & K. J. Sher (Eds.), *APA handbook of research methods in psychology. Research designs: Quantitative, qualitative, neuropsychological, and biological* (2nd ed., pp. 285–304). American Psychological Association.

Gone, J. P., & Calf Looking, P. E. (2015). The Blackfeet Indian culture camp: Auditioning an alternative indigenous treatment for substance use disorders. *Psychological Services, 12*(2), 83–91.

Goodley, D. & Runswick-Cole, K. (2012). Decolonizing methodology: Disabled children as research managers and participant ethnographers. In A. Azzopardi & S. Grech (Eds.), *Inclusive communities: A critical reader* (pp. 215–232). Sense Publishers.

Goodman, L. A., Epstein, D., & Sullivan, C. M. (2018). Beyond the RCT: Integrating rigor and relevance to evaluate the outcomes of domestic violence programs. *American Journal of Evaluation, 39*(1), 58–70.

Goodman, R. D., & Gorski, P. C. (Eds.) (2014). *Decolonizing "multicultural" counseling through social justice*. Springer.

Goodman, L. A., Litwin, A., Bohlig, A., Weintraub, S. R., Green, A. Walker, J., White, L., & Ryan, N. (2007). Applying feminist theory to community practice: A case example of a multi-level empowerment intervention for low-income women with depression. In E. Aldarando (Ed.), *Promoting social justice through mental health practice* (pp. 265–290). Lawrence Erlbaum Associates.

Goodman, A., Morgan, R., Kuehlke, R., Kastor, S., Fleming, K., & Boyd, J. (2018). "We've been researched to death": Exploring the research experiences of urban Indigenous peoples in Vancouver, Canada. *International Indigenous Policy Journal, 9*(2), 1–20.

Goodman, L. A., Thomas, K. A., Nnawulezi, N., Lippy, C., Serrata, J. V., Ghanbarpour, S. Sullivan, C., & Bair-Merritt, M. H. (2018). Bringing community based participatory research to domestic violence scholarship: An online toolkit. *Journal of Family Violence, 33*(2), 103–107.

Goodman, L. A., Thomas, K. A., Serrata, J. V., Lippy, C., Nnawulezi, N., Ghanbarpour, S., Sullivan, S. & Bair-Merritt, M.H. (2017). *Bringing community based participatory research to intimate partner violence research: A toolkit for emerging researchers*. National Resource Center on Domestic Violence. Available at https://cbprtoolkit.org/.

Gordon, R. (2019). "Why would I want to be anonymous?" Questioning ethical principles of anonymity in cross-cultural feminist research. *Gender & Development, 27*(3), 541–554.

Goto, A., Iwakabe, S., & Heim, N. (2022). Therapeutic courage in novice therapists in Japan: A qualitative study. *Journal of Psychotherapy Integration, 32*(3), 243–256.

Graeber, D., & Wengrow, D. (2021). *The dawn of everything: A new history of humanity*. Penguin.

Granek, L. (2017). Emotional aspects of conducting qualitative research on psychological topics. *Qualitative Psychology, 4*(3), 281–286.

Granek, L., & Nakash, O. (2016). The impact of qualitative research on the "real world" knowledge translation as education, policy, clinical training, and clinical practice. *Journal of Humanistic Psychology, 56*(4), 414–435.

Gregersen, T. A., Birkelund, R., Wolderslund, M., Steffensen, K. D., & Ammentorp, J. (2022). When life gives you no choice: Context of decision-making when offered an oncology clinical trial. *Scandinavian Journal of Caring Sciences, 36*(1), 81–89.

Griffiths, K., Diaz, A., Whop, L. J., & Cunningham, J. (2022). The health and wellbeing of indigenous and tribal peoples around the globe: Ensuring and promoting best practice in research. *International Journal of Environmental Research and Public Health, 19*(1), 261–273.

Groot, B. C., & Abma, T. A. (2020). Participatory health research with mothers living in poverty in the Netherlands: Pathways and challenges to strengthen empowerment. *Forum Qualitative Sozialforschung/Forum: Qualitative Social Research, 21*(1). https://doi.org/10.17169/fqs-21.1.3302

Groot, B., Haveman, A., & Abma, T. (2022). Relational, ethically sound co-production in mental health care research: Epistemic injustice and the need for an ethics of care. *Critical Public Health, 32*(2), 230–240.

Groot, B. C., Schrijver, J., & Abma, T. A. (2021). Are you afraid of press and social media? Ethics in photovoice in participatory health research. *Educational Action Research*, 1–19. https://doi.org/10.1080/09650792.2021.1941164

Groot, B. C., Vink, M., Haveman, A., Huberts, M., Schout, G., & Abma, T. A. (2019). Ethics of care in participatory health research: Mutual responsibility in collaboration with co-researchers. *Educational Action Research, 27*(2), 286–302.

Guenther, K. M. (2009). The politics of names: Rethinking the methodological and ethical significance of naming people, organizations, and places. *Qualitative Research, 9*(4), 411–421.

Guillemin, M., & Gillam, L. (2004). Ethics, reflexivity and ethically important moments in research. *Qualitative Inquiry, 10*, 261–280.

Guillemin, M., & Heggen, K. (2009). Rapport and respect: Negotiating ethical relations between researcher and participant. *Medicine, Health Care and Philosophy, 12*(3), 291–299.

Guishard, M. (2009). The false paths, the endless labors, the turns now this way and now that: Participatory action research, mutual vulnerability, and the politics of inquiry. *The Urban Review, 41*(1), 85–105.

Gupta, N. (2021). Harnessing phenomenological research to facilitate conscientização about oppressive lived experience. *Journal of Humanistic Psychology, 61*(6), 906–924.

Hallett, J., Held, S., McCormick, A. K. H. G., Simonds, V., Real Bird, S., Martin, C., ... & Trottier, C. (2017). What touched your heart? Collaborative story analysis emerging from an Apsáalooke cultural context. *Qualitative Health Research, 27*(9), 1267–1277.

Hallett, S. & Kerr, C. (2020). *"You need support, validation, good coping skills. You need and deserve acceptance": Autistic Adult Experiences of Counselling.* Autistic Mental Health & Autistic Mutual Aid Society Edinburgh (AMASE). (accessed on 21st February 2023 from www.autisticmentalhealth.uk/counsellingreport)

Halling, S. (2005). When intimacy and companionship are at the core of the phenomenological research process. *Indo-Pacific Journal of Phenomenology, 5*(1), 1–11.

Hanley, T., Sefi, A., Grauberg, J., Prescott, J., & Etchebarne, A. (2021). A theory of change for web-based therapy and support services for children and young people: Collaborative qualitative exploration. *JMIR Pediatrics and Parenting, 4*(1), e23193.

Hansford, L., Thomas, F., & Wyatt, K. (2019). The impact of the Work Capability Assessment on mental health: Claimants' lived experiences and GP perspectives in low-income communities. *Journal of Poverty and Social Justice, 27*(3), 351–368.

Harding, S., & Norberg, K. (2005). New feminist approaches to social science methodologies: An introduction. *Signs, 30*, 2009–2015.

Harris, P., Ellem, K., Gallagher, H., Burgess, A., Abson, L., Sunderland, N., & The Queenslander Self-Advocates. (2024). Building capacity to engage in co-produced research: Reflections from a digital storytelling project. *Disability & Society, 39*(5), 1256–1275.

Harris, T., Lepper, G., Cheetham, B., Crowther, C., King, D., & Ryde, J. (2020). Bridging the gap between clinical practice and research Part I: Findings of a pilot study on Daniel Stern's 'Moments of Meeting' from the UKCP's Practitioner Research Network. *British Journal of Psychotherapy, 36*(2), 180–199.

Hartogs, B. M. A., Eikmans, K. M., & Bartels-Velthuis, A. A. (2012). Melting down the Ice Queen: An integrative treatment of anorexia nervosa. *BMJ Case Reports.* Published online. doi:10.1136/bcr-2012- 006604

Heaton, J. (2022). "*Pseudonyms are used throughout": A footnote, unpacked. *Qualitative Inquiry*, *28*(1), 123–132.

Heney, V., & Poleykett, B. (2022). The impossibility of engaged research: Complicity and accountability between researchers, 'publics' and institutions. *Sociology of Health & Illness*, *44*, 179–194.

Hernández, K. J., Rubis, J. M., Theriault, N., Todd, Z., Mitchell, A., Country, B., ... & Wright, S. (2021). The creatures collective: Manifestings. *Environment and Planning E: Nature and Space*, *4*(3), 838–863.

Hersted, L., Ness, O., & Frimann, S. (Eds.) (2019). *Action research in a relational perspective: Dialogue, reflexivity, power and ethics*. Routledge.

Hess, J. M., Vasquez Guzman, C. E., Hernandez-Vallant, A., Handal, A. J., Huyser, K., Galvis, M., Medina, D., Casas, N., Chavez, M. J., Carreon Fuentes, A., & Goodkind, J. R. (2022). Innovative participatory bilingual data analysis with Latinx/@ immigrants: Language, power, and transformation. *Cultural Diversity and Ethnic Minority Psychology*, *28*(3), 389–401.

Hodgins, M., & McNamara, P. M. (2019). An enlightened environment? Workplace bullying and incivility in Irish higher education. *Sage Open*, *9*(4), 2158244019894278.

Hoggett, P., Lousada, J., Maguire, M., & Ryan, J. (2022). Battersea Action and Counselling Centre (BACC). *Psychoanalysis and History*, *24*(3), 291–298.

Hokowhitu, B., Moreton-Robinson, A., Tuhiwai-Smith, L., Andersen, C., & Larkin, S. (Eds.) (2022). *Routledge handbook of critical indigenous studies*. Routledge.

Holland, S. (1992). From social abuse to social action: A neighborhood psychotherapy and social action project for women. In J. Ussher & P. Nicholson (Eds.), *Gender Issues in Clinical Psychology* (pp. 68–77). Routledge.

Huet, V., Springham, N., & Evans, C. (2014). The art therapy practice research network: Hurdles, pitfalls and achievements. *Counselling & Psychotherapy Research*, *14*(3), 174–180.

Hughes, M., & Barlo, S. (2021). Yarning with country: An indigenist research methodology. *Qualitative Inquiry*, *27*(3–4), 353–363.

Hundt, G. L., Stuttaford, M. C., Bryanston, C., & Harrison, C. (2019). "Research usually sits on shelves, through the play it was shared." Co-producing knowledge through post-show discussions of research-based theatre. *Frontiers in Sociology*, *4*, 48.

Illarregi, E. R. (2021). *Co-design as healing: Exploring the experiences of participants facing mental health problems*. PhD Thesis. Open University (United Kingdom).

Illarregi, E. R., Alexiou, K., DiMalta, G., & Zamenopoulos, T. (2023). Is designing therapeutic? A case study exploring the experience of co-design and psychosis. *Psychosis*, *15*(3), 277–291.

Ingold, T. (2005). On the social relations of the hunter-gatherer band. In R. B. Lee & R. Daly (Eds.), *The Cambridge Encyclopedia of Hunters and Gatherers* (pp. 399–410). Cambridge University Press.

Ito-Jaeger, S., Perez Vallejos, E., Curran, T., & Crawford, P. (2022). What's up with everyone? A qualitative study on young people's perceptions of cocreated online animations to promote mental health literacy. *Health Expectations*, *25*(4), 1633–1642.

Iwasaki, Y., Springett, J., Dashora, P., McLaughlin, A. M., McHugh, T. L., & Youth 4 YEG Team. (2014). Youth-guided youth engagement: Participatory action research (PAR) with high-risk, marginalized youth. *Child & Youth Services*, *35*(4), 316–342.

Jennings, B. (2016). Reconceptualizing autonomy: A relational turn in bioethics. *Hastings Center Report*, *46*, 11–16.

Jennings, B. (2018). Solidarity and care as relational practices. *Bioethics*, *32*, 553–561.

Jennings, H., Slade, M., Bates, P., Munday, E., & Toney, R. (2018). Best practice framework for Patient and Public Involvement (PPI) in collaborative data analysis of qualitative mental health research: Methodology development and refinement. *BMC Psychiatry*, *18*(1), 1–11.

Johnson, R. B. (2017). Dialectical pluralism: A metaparadigm whose time has come. *Journal of Mixed Methods Research, 11*(2), 156–173.

Johnson, R. B. (2024). Dialectical pluralism and integration in mixed methods research. In Y. Shan (Ed.), *Philosophical Foundations of Mixed Methods Research* (pp. 100–126). Routledge.

Johnson, W., & Parry, D. (Eds.) (2022). *Fostering social justice through qualitative inquiry*. 2nd edn. Routledge.

Jones, B., & Hunt, A. (2022). Collaboration between doctoral researchers and patient research partners: Reflections and considerations. *Research for All, 6*(1), 2, 1–9.

Jones, P., Cedar, L., Coleman, A., Haythorne, D., Mercieca, D., & Ramsden, E. (2020). *Child agency and voice in therapy: New ways of working in the arts therapies*. Routledge.

Josselson, R. (1996). On writing other people's lives, self-analytic reflections of a narrative researcher. In R. Josselson (Ed.), *Ethics and Process in the Narrative Study of Lives* (pp. 60–71). Sage.

Katz-Wise, S. L., Pullen Sansfaçon, A., Bogart, L. M., Rosal, M. C., Ehrensaft, D., Goldman, R. E., & Bryn Austin, S. (2019). Lessons from a community-based participatory research study with transgender and gender nonconforming youth and their families. *Action Research, 17*(2), 186–207.

Kaulino, A., & Matus, T. (2021). Theoretical proposal for the relationship between epistemology and ethics in psychology. *Theory & Psychology, 31*(2), 237–253.

Keetharuth, A. D., Brazier, J., Connell, J., Bjorner, J. B., Carlton, J., Buck, E. T., ... & Barkham, M. (2018). Recovering Quality of Life (ReQoL): A new generic self-reported outcome measure for use with people experiencing mental health difficulties. *The British Journal of Psychiatry, 212*(1), 42–49.

Kennedy, S., Bewley, S., Chevous, J., Perôt, C., Vigneri, M., & Bacchus, L. J. (2022). A systematic review that evaluates the extent and quality of involving childhood abuse survivors in shaping, conducting and disseminating research in the UK. *Research for All, 6*(1), 3, 1–25.

Kidd, S. A., & Kral, M. J. (2005). Practicing participatory action research. *Journal of Counseling Psychology, 52*, 187–195.

Kinney, P. (2017). Walking interviews. *Social Research Update, 67*, 1–4.

Kinney, P. (2021). Walking interviews: A novel way of ensuring the voices of vulnerable populations are included in research. In M. Borcsa & C. Willig (Eds.), *Qualitative research methods in mental health: Innovative and collaborative approaches* (pp. 65–82). Springer.

Klein, M., & Milner, R. J. (2019). The use of body-mapping in interpretative phenomenological analyses: A methodological discussion. *International Journal of Social Research Methodology, 22*(5), 533–543.

Klocker, N. (2015). Participatory action research: The distress of (not) making a difference. *Emotion, Space and Society, 17*, 37–44.

Knowles, S., Sharma, V., Fortune, S., Wadman, R., Churchill, R., & Hetrick, S. (2022). Adapting a codesign process with young people to prioritize outcomes for a systematic review of interventions to prevent self-harm and suicide. *Health Expectations, 25*(4), 1393–1404.

Kuriloff, P. J., Andrus, S. H., & Ravitch, S. M. (2011). Messy ethics: Conducting moral participatory action research in the crucible of university–school relations. *Mind, Brain, and Education, 5*(2), 49–62.

Lahman, M. K., Thomas, R., & Teman, E. D. (2023). A good name: Pseudonyms in research. *Qualitative Inquiry, 29*(6), 678–685.

Lakeman, R., McAndrew, S., MacGabhann, L., & Warne, T. (2013). 'That was helpful… no one has talked to me about that before': Research participation as a therapeutic activity. *International Journal of Mental Health Nursing, 22*(1), 76–84.

Lambert, N., & Carr, S. (2018). "Outside the Original Remit": Co-production in UK mental health research, lessons from the field. *International Journal of Mental Health Nursing, 27*(4), 1273–1281.

Larsen, H., Friis, P., Hvidt, E. A., Hvidt, N. C., Timmermann, C., Sørensen, L., & Ammentorp, J. (2018). From theatre improvisation to video scenes - what are the implications for the quality of existential conversation? *Participatory Innovation Conference* (pp. 87–94). Malardalen University, Sweden.

Lauzon-Schnittka, J., Audette-Chapdelaine, S., Boutin, D., Wilhelmy, C., Auger, A. M., & Brodeur, M. (2022). The experience of patient partners in research: A qualitative systematic review and thematic synthesis. *Research Involvement and Engagement, 8*(1), 1–22.

Lave, J., & Wenger, E. (1991). *Legitimate Peripheral participation in communities of practice. Situated learning.* Cambridge University Press.

Lea, L., Byford, S., Coney, Y., Crane, R., Fagabemi, N., Gurney, T., Leigh-Phippard, H., Rosten, C., Simms, K., & Strauss, C. (2020). Reflections on my role as a mental health service user co-applicant in a randomized control trial. *Research for All, 4*(1), 33–46.

Lehr, R., Belgrave, M., Watt, C., & Hill-Lehr, A. (2013). Ethical discernment points: The alchemy of dialogue, deliberation, and decisions. *Canadian Journal of Counselling and Psychotherapy, 47*(4), 441-459.

Lenette, C. (2021). Health on the move: Walking interviews in health and wellbeing research. In D. Lupton & D. Leahy (Eds.), *Creative approaches to health education: New ways of thinking, making, doing, teaching and learning* (pp. 136–159). Routledge.

Lenette, C., Stavropoulou, N., Nunn, C., Kong, S. T., Cook, T., Coddington, K., & Banks, S. (2019). Brushed under the carpet: Examining the complexities of participatory research. *Research for All, 3*(2), 161–179.

Levitt, H. M., Ipekci, B., Morrill, Z., & Rizo, J. L. (2021a). Intersubjective recognition as the methodological enactment of epistemic privilege: A critical basis for consensus and intersubjective confirmation procedures. *Qualitative Psychology, 8*(3), 407–427.

Levitt, H. M., Morrill, Z., Collins, K. M., & Rizo, J. L. (2021b). The methodological integrity of critical qualitative research: Principles to support design and research review. *Journal of Counseling Psychology, 68*(3), 357–372.

Levitt, H. M., Surace, F. I., Wu, M. B., Chapin, B., Hargrove, J. G., Herbitter, C., Lu, E. C., Maroney, M. R., & Hochman, A. L. (2022). The meaning of scientific objectivity and subjectivity: From the perspective of methodologists. *Psychological Methods, 27*(4), 589–605.

Liamputtong, P. & Rice, Z. S. (2021). Participatory research: Coproduction of knowledge as inclusive research. In P. Liamputtong (Ed.), *Handbook of social inclusion* (pp. 1–17). Springer.

Lieblich, A. (2006). Vicissitudes: A study, a book, a play: Lessons from the work of a narrative scholar. *Qualitative Inquiry, 12*(1), 60–80.

Lieblich, A. (2013). Healing plots: Writing and reading in life-stories groups. *Qualitative Inquiry, 19*(1), 46–52.

Lindquist-Grantz, R., Downing, K., Hicks, M., Houchin, C., & Ackman, V. (2022). The benefits of peer interviewers in research: Evidence from a youth homelessness longitudinal evaluation study. *Collaborations: A Journal of Community-Based Research and Practice, 5*(1). https://doi.org/10.33596/ coll.83

Litz, B. T., Stein, N., Delaney, E., Lebowitz, L., Nash, W. P., Silva, C., & Maguen, S. (2009). Moral injury and moral repair in war veterans: A preliminary model and intervention strategy. *Clinical Psychology Review, 29*(8), 695–706.

Locock, L., Boylan, A. M., Snow, R., & Staniszewska, S. (2017). The power of symbolic capital in patient and public involvement in health research. *Health Expectations, 20*(5), 836–844.

Locock, L., Kirkpatrick, S., Brading, L., Sturmey, G., Cornwell, J., Churchill, N., & Robert, G. (2019). Involving service users in the qualitative analysis of patient narratives to support healthcare quality improvement. *Research Involvement and Engagement*, *5*, 1–11.

Lott, D. A. (2000). *In session: The bond between women and their therapists*. W.H. Freeman.

Loveridge, J., Wood, B. E., Davis-Rae, E., & McRae, H. (2024). Ethical challenges in participatory research with children and youth. *Qualitative Research*, *24*(2), 391–411.

Lynch, K., Kalaitzake, M., & Crean, M. (2021). Care and affective relations: Social justice and sociology. *The Sociological Review*, *69*(1), 53–71.

MacFarlane, A., & LeMaster, J. (2022). Disrupting patterns of exclusion in participatory spaces: Involving people from vulnerable populations. *Health Expectations: An International Journal of Public Participation in Health Care and Health Policy*, *25*(5), 2031.

Mackrill, T. (2007). Using a cross-contextual qualitative diary design to explore client experiences of psychotherapy. *Counselling & Psychotherapy Research*, *7*, 233–239.

Mackrill, T. (2008a). Solicited diary studies of psychotherapeutic practice – pros and cons. *European Journal of Psychotherapy and Counselling*, 10, 5–18.

Mackrill, T. (2008b). Exploring psychotherapy clients' independent strategies for change while in therapy. *British Journal of Guidance & Counselling*, *36*(4), 441–453.

Mackrill, T. (2008c). Pre-treatment change in psychotherapy with adult children of problem drinkers: The significance of leaving home. *Counselling and Psychotherapy Research*, *8*(3), 160–165.

Mackrill, T. (2011). A diary-based, cross-contextual case study methodology: Background for the case of "Jane and Joe". *Pragmatic Case Studies in Psychotherapy*, *7*(1), 156–186.

Madden, A., Lennon, P., Hogan, C., Getty, M., Hopwood, M., Neale, J., & Treloar, C. (2019). Patient-reported measures as a justice project through involvement of service-user researchers. In P. Aggleton, A. Broom, & J. Moss (Eds.) *Practical Justice: Principles, Practice and Social Change* (pp. 190–199). Routledge.

Maguire, K., & Britten, N. (2017). "How can anybody be representative for those kind of people?" Forms of patient representation in health research, and why it is always contestable. *Social Science & Medicine*, *183*, 62–69.

Maguire, K., & Britten, N. (2018). "You're there because you are unprofessional": Patient and public involvement as liminal knowledge spaces. *Sociology of Health & Illness*, *40*(3), 463–477.

Mann, J., & Hung, L. (2019). Co-research with people living with dementia for change. *Action Research*, *17*(4), 573–590.

Marcotte, J., Grandisson, M., Milot, É., & Dupéré, S. (2022). The walking interview: A promising method for promoting the participation of autistic people in research projects. *International Journal of Qualitative Methods*, *21*, 16094069221090065.

Marino, C. K. (2015). To belong, contribute, and hope: First stage development of a measure of social recovery. *Journal of Mental Health*, *24*(2), 68–72.

Matheson, C., & Weightman, E. (2021a). A participatory study of patient views on psychotherapy for complex post-traumatic stress disorder, CPTSD. *Journal of Mental Health*, *30*(6), 690–697.

Matheson, C., & Weightman, E. (2021b). Research and recovery: Can patient participation in research promote recovery for people with complex post-traumatic stress disorder, CPTSD? *Health Expectations*, *24*, 62–69.

Mayer, C., & McKenzie, K. (2017). "… it shows that there's no limits": The psychological impact of co-production for experts by experience working in youth mental health. *Health & Social Care in the Community*, *25*(3), 1181–1189.

McConnell, T., Best, P., Davidson, G., McEneaney, T., Cantrell, C., & Tully, M. (2018). Coproduction for feasibility and pilot randomised controlled trials: Learning outcomes for community partners, service users and the research team. *Research Involvement and Engagement, 4*(1), 1–11.

McDonald, L. E., & Capous-Desyllas, M. (2021). Navigating ethical issues in photovoice: Balancing the principles of community-based participatory research ethics with Institutional Review Board requirements. *Journal of Empirical Research on Human Research Ethics, 16*(4), 364–373.

McEvoy, P. M., Horgan, B., Eadon, O. L., Yong, M. J., Soraine, J., & Chiu, V. W. (2023). Development of a research capacity and culture tool for people with lived experience of mental health challenges. *Australian & New Zealand Journal of Psychiatry, 57*(6), 865–874.

McGoey, L. (2010). Profitable failure: Antidepressant drugs and the triumph of flawed experiments. *History of the Human Sciences, 23*(1), 58–78.

McGoey, L. (2019). *The unknowers: How strategic ignorance rules the world.* Zed Books.

McKillop, J., & Wilkinson, H. (2004). Make it easy on yourself! Advice to researchers from someone with dementia on being interviewed. *Dementia, 3*(2), 117–125.

McLeod, J. (2011). *Qualitative research in counselling and psychotherapy*. 2nd edn. Sage.

McLeod, J. (2016). *Using research in counselling and psychotherapy*. Sage.

McLeod, J. (2017). Science and psychotherapy: Developing research-based knowledge that enhances the effectiveness of practice. *Transactional Analysis Journal, 47*(2), 82–101.

McLeod, J. (2018). *Pluralistic therapy: Distinctive features*. Routledge.

McLeod, J. (2022) *Doing research in counselling and psychotherapy.* 4th edn. Sage.

McLeod, J., & Sundet, R. (2022). Psychotherapy as making. *Frontiers in Psychology, 13*, 1048665.

McPherson, S., & Beresford, P. (2019). Semantics of patient choice: how the UK national guideline for depression silences patients. *Disability & Society, 34*(3), 491–497.

McPherson, S. (2020). A NICE game of Minecraft: philosophical flaws underpinning UK depression guideline nosology. *Medical Humanities, 46*(3), 162–165.

McPherson, S., Rost, F., Sidhu, S., & Dennis, M. (2020). Non-strategic ignorance: Considering the potential for a paradigm shift in evidence-based mental health. *Health, 24*(1), 3–20.

Mehl-Madrona, L., & Pennycook, G. (2009). Construction of an aboriginal theory of mind and mental health. *Anthropology of Consciousness, 20*(2), 85–100.

Melluish, S., & Bulmer, D. (1999). Rebuilding solidarity: An account of a men's health action project. *Journal of Community and Applied Social Psychology, 9*, 93–100.

Millett, L., Taylor, B. L., Howard, L. M., Bick, D., Stanley, N., & Johnson, S. (2018). Experiences of improving access to psychological therapy services for perinatal mental health difficulties: A qualitative study of women's and therapists' views. *Behavioural and Cognitive Psychotherapy, 46*(4), 421–436.

Mind. (2013). *We still need to talk: A report on access to talking therapies.* Mind London. https://www.mind.org.uk/media-a/4248/we-still-need-to-talk_report.pdf (accessed 12th February 2023).

Montgomery, L., Kelly, B., Campbell, U., Davidson, G., Gibson, L., Hughes, L., ... & Wood, L. (2022). Getting our voices heard in research: A review of peer researcher's roles and experiences on a qualitative study of adult safeguarding policy. *Research Involvement and Engagement, 8*(1), 1–12.

Moradi, B., & Grzanka, P. R. (2017). Using intersectionality responsibly: Toward critical epistemology, structural analysis, and social justice activism. *Journal of Counseling Psychology, 64*, 500–513.

Morgan, G., Barnwell, G., Johnstone, L., Shukla, K., & Mitchell, A. (2022). The power threat meaning framework and the climate and ecological crises. *PINS, 63*, 83–109.

Morley, G., Ives, J., & Bradbury-Jones, C. (2019). Moral distress and austerity: An avoidable ethical challenge in healthcare. *Health Care Analysis*, *27*, 185–201.

Morris, M., & Davies, A. (2018). Being both researcher and subject: Attending to emotion within collaborative inquiry. In T. Loughran & D. Mannay (Eds.), *Emotion and the researcher: Sites, subjectivities, and relationships* (pp. 229–244). Emerald Publishing.

Morrow, S. (2006). Honor and respect: Feminist collaborative research with sexually abused women. In C. T. Fischer (Ed.), *Qualitative research methods for psychologists: Introduction through empirical examples* (pp. 143–172). Academic Press.

Morrow, S. L. (2009). A journey into survival and coping by women survivors of childhood sexual abuse. In L. Finlay & K. Evans (Eds.), *Relational-centred research for psychotherapists: Exploring meanings and experiences* (pp. 227–239). Wiley-Blackwell.

Morrow, S. L., & Smith, M. L. (1995). Constructions of survival and coping by women who have survived childhood sexual abuse. *Journal of Counseling Psychology*, *42*, 24–33.

Murphy, K., Jordan, F., Hunter, A., Cooney, A., & Casey, D. (2015). Articulating the strategies for maximising the inclusion of people with dementia in qualitative research studies. *Dementia*, *14*(6), 800–824.

Nadeau, L., Gaulin, D., Johnson-Lafleur, J., Levesque, C., & Fraser, S. (2022). The challenges of decolonising participatory research in indigenous contexts: The Atautsikut community of practice experience in Nunavik. *International Journal of Circumpolar Health*, *81*(1), 2087846.

National Institute for Health and Care Research (2021). Briefing notes for researchers - public involvement in NHS, health and social care research. https://www.nihr.ac.uk/documents/briefing-notes-for-researchers-public-involvement-in-nhs-health-and-social-care-research/27371#ethics (accessed 13th February 2023).

Neale, J., Tompkins, C., Wheeler, C., Finch, E., Marsden, J., Mitcheson, L., ... & Strang, J. (2015). "You're all going to hate the word 'recovery' by the end of this": Service users' views of measuring addiction recovery. *Drugs: Education, Prevention and Policy*, *22*(1), 26–34.

Nieder, T. O., & Strauss, B. (2015). Transgender health care in Germany: Participatory approaches and the development of a guideline. *International Review of Psychiatry*, *27*(5), 416–426.

Norcross, J. C. & Cooper, M. (2021). *Personalizing psychotherapy: Assessing and accommodating patient preferences.* American Psychological Association.

Novek, S., & Wilkinson, H. (2019). Safe and inclusive research practices for qualitative research involving people with dementia: A review of key issues and strategies. *Dementia*, *18*(3), 1042–1059.

Novis-Deutsch, N. (2020). Pluralism as an antidote to epistemic violence in psychological research. *Theory & Psychology*, *30*(3), 408–413.

Nussbaum, M. (2011). *Creating capabilities: The human development approach.* Harvard University Press.

Oakley, L., Fenge, L., & Taylor, B. (2022). "I call it the hero complex" – Critical considerations of power and privilege and seeking to be an agent of change in qualitative researchers' experiences. *Qualitative Research in Psychology*, *19*(3), 587–561.

Oaks, L., Israel, T., Conover, K. J., Cogger, A., & Avellar, T. R. (2019). Community-based participatory research with invisible, geographically-dispersed communities: Partnering with lesbian, gay, bisexual, transgender and queer communities on the California central coast. *Journal for Social Action in Counseling & Psychology*, *11*(1), 14–32.

Oddli, H. W., Stänicke, E., Halvorsen, M. S., & Lindstad, T. G. (2023). Causality in psychotherapy research: Towards evidential pluralism. *Psychotherapy Research*, *33*(8), 1004–1018.

Ogrodniczuk, J. S., Cheek, J., & Kealy, D. (2021). Group therapy development: Implications for nontherapy groups. In C. D. Parks & G. A. Tasca (Eds.), *The psychology of groups: The intersection of social psychology and psychotherapy research* (pp. 231–248). American Psychological Association.

Olsen, A., & Carter, C. (2016). Responding to the needs of people with learning disabilities who have been raped: Co-production in action. *Tizard Learning Disability Review*, *21*(1), 30–38.

Ostrom, E. (1990). *Governing the commons: The evolution of institutions for collective action*. Cambridge University Press.

Page, K. (2022). Ethics and the co-production of knowledge. *Public Health Research and Practice*, *32*(2), 1–5.

Panofsky, S., Buchanan, M. J., Wilat, T. A. Z., Madeek, D. Z., Neekupdeh, D. Z., Smogelgem, D. Z., ... & John, R. (2023). The Wet'suwet'en Nation's mobilization of indigenous focusing oriented therapy: An exploratory study. *The Counseling Psychologist*, *51*(3), 333–367.

Parker, M., Wallerstein, N., Duran, B., Magarati, M., Burgess, E., Sanchez-Youngman, S., ... & Koegel, P. (2020). Engage for equity: Development of community-based participatory research tools. *Health Education & Behavior*, *47*(3), 359–371.

Pastor, S. (2020). Decentred evaluation that empowers: Incorporating a double-storied approach to evaluation interviewing and story production. *International Journal of Narrative Therapy & Community Work*, 3, 50–57.

Patel, P., Kennedy, A., Carr, S., Gillard, S., Harris, P., & Sweeney, A. (2022). Service user experiences of mental health assessments: A systematic review and thematic synthesis of qualitative literature. *Journal of Mental Health*, 1–14. https://doi.org/10.1080/09638237.2022.2069691

Patel, T. (2020). Research in therapeutic practice settings: Ethical considerations. In R. Tribe & J. Morrissey (Eds.), *The Handbook of professional ethical and research practice for psychologists, counsellors, psychotherapists and psychiatrists*. 3rd edn (pp. 191–205). Routledge.

Patton, P., & Moss, J. (2019). Concepts of justice and practical injustices. In P. Aggleton, A. Broom, & J. Moss (Eds.), *Practical justice: Principles, practice and social change* (pp. 9–24). Routledge.

Pavarini, G., Booysen, C., Jain, T., Lai, J., Manku, K., Foster-Estwick, A., ... & Singh, I. (2023). Agents of change for mental health: A survey of young people's aspirations for participation across five low-and middle-income countries. *Journal of Adolescent Health*, *72*(1), S96–S104.

Pavarini, G., Lorimer, J., Manzini, A., Goundrey-Smith, E., & Singh, I. (2019). Co-producing research with youth: The NeurOx young people's advisory group model. *Health Expectations*, *22*(4), 743–751.

Pavarini, G., Smith, L. M., Shaughnessy, N., Mankee-Williams, A., Thirumalai, J. K., Russell, N., & Bhui, K. (2021). Ethical issues in participatory arts methods for young people with adverse childhood experiences. *Health Expectations*, *24*(5), 1557–1569.

Pellicano, E., Lawson, W., Hall, G., Mahony, J., Lilley, R., Heyworth, M., ... & Yudell, M. (2022). "I knew she'd get it, and get me": Participants' perspectives of a participatory autism research project. *Autism in Adulthood*, *4*(2), 120–129.

Perry, S., Carpenter, S., & CLEAR IDEAS. (2016). Preliminary development and piloting of a user-generated routine outcome measure in a children and young people's counselling service. *Counselling and Psychotherapy Research*, *16*(3), 171–182.

Pham, T. V., Pomerville, A., Burrage, R. L., & Gone, J. P. (2024). An interview-based evaluation of an Indigenous traditional spirituality program at an urban American Indian health clinic. *Transcultural Psychiatry*, 61(3), 488–503.

Phillips, L. J., Larsen, A., & Mengel, L. (2022). What "coproduction" in participatory research means from participants' perspectives: A collaborative autoethnographic inquiry. *Journal of Participatory Research Methods*, *3*(2), 1.

Pichon, L. C., Teti, M., & Brown, L. L. (2022). Triggers or prompts? When methods resurface unsafe memories and the value of trauma-informed photovoice research practices. *International Journal of Qualitative Methods, 21*, 16094069221113979.

Polansky, L., Ferronato, H., & Herbert, J. (2022). Listening with the heart: A reflection on relationality and ceremony. *Canadian Journal of Program Evaluation, 37*(2), 283-290.

Pollock, A., Campbell, P., Struthers, C., Synnot, A., Nunn, J., Hill, S., ... & Morley, R. (2019). Development of the ACTIVE framework to describe stakeholder involvement in systematic reviews. *Journal of Health Services Research & Policy, 24*(4), 245–255.

Pomerville, A., Kawennison Fetter, A., & Gone, J. P. (2022). American Indian behavioral health treatment preferences as perceived by Urban Indian Health Program providers. *Qualitative Health Research, 32*(3), 465–478.

Pratt, B. (2019a). Engagement as co-constructing knowledge: A moral necessity in public health research. *Bioethics, 33*(7), 805–813.

Pratt, B. (2019b). Constructing citizen engagement in health research priority-setting to attend to dynamics of power and difference. *Developing World Bioethics, 19*(1), 45–60.

Pratt, B. (2021a). What are important ways of sharing power in health research priority setting? Perspectives from people with lived experience and members of the public. *Journal of Empirical Research on Human Research Ethics, 16*(3), 200–211.

Pratt, B. (2021b). Sharing power in global health research: An ethical toolkit for designing priority-setting processes that meaningfully include communities. *International Journal for Equity in Health, 20*(1), 1–11.

Pratt, B., Seshadri, T., & Srinivas, P. N. (2022). Overcoming structural barriers to sharing power with communities in global health research priority-setting: Lessons from the Participation for Local Action project in Karnataka, India. *Global Public Health, 17*(12), 3334–3352.

Prinds, C., Timmerman, C., Hvidtjørn, D., Ammentorp, J., Hvidt, N. C., Larsen, H., & Viftrup, D. T. (2021). Existential aspects in the transition to parenthood based on interviews and a theatre workshop. *Sexual & Reproductive Healthcare, 28*, 100612.

Råbu, M., McLeod, J., Haavind, H., Bernhardt, I. S., Nissen-Lie, H., & Moltu, C. (2021). How psychotherapists make use of their experiences from being a client: Lessons from a collective autoethnography. *Counselling Psychology Quarterly, 34*(1), 109–128.

Rand, J. R., Melro, C., Biderman, M., McMillan, L. J., Miller, A. D., Lekas, S., & Numer, M. (2023). Indigenous men's pathways to "living the right kind of life and walking the right path" post incarceration in Canada: Understanding the impacts of systemic oppression, and guidance for healing and (w)holistic sexual health. *Culture, Health & Sexuality, 25*(4), 475–489.

Rasras, K. (2005). A human rights approach to psychotherapy. *International Journal of Narrative Therapy & Community Work*, 3/4, 57–60.

Redvers, N., Celidwen, Y., Schultz, C., Horn, O., Githaiga, C., Vera, M., ... & Rojas, J. N. (2022). The determinants of planetary health: An Indigenous consensus perspective. *The Lancet Planetary Health, 6*(2), e156–e163.

Reeves, A., & Bond, T. (2021). *Standards and Ethics for Counselling in Action.* 5th edn. Sage.

Reeves, A., & Stewart, S. (2017). Healing the spirit: Exploring sexualized trauma and recovery among Indigenous men in Toronto. *American Indian and Alaska Native Mental Health Research, 24*(1), 30–60.

Reynolds, J., & Beresford, R. (2020). "An active, productive life": Narratives of, and through, participation in Public and Patient Involvement in Health Research. *Qualitative Health Research, 30*(14), 2265–2277.

Robbins, R. R., Hill, J., & McWhirter, P. T. (2008). Conflicting epistemologies: A case study of a traditional American Indian in therapy. *Clinical Case Studies, 7*(5), 449–466.

Robinson, J. (2018). Participatory research with adults with Asperger's syndrome in the UK. In S. Banks & M. Brydon-Miller (Eds.), *Ethics in participatory research for health and social well-being* (pp. 43–46). Routledge.

Rodríguez Espinosa, P., Sussman, A., Pearson, C. R., Oetzel, J. G., & Wallerstein, N. (2020). Personal outcomes in community-based participatory research partnerships: A cross-site mixed methods study. *American Journal of Community Psychology*, *66*(3–4), 439–449.

Rodriguez Espinosa, P. R., & Verney, S. P. (2021). The underutilization of community-based participatory research in psychology: A systematic review. *American Journal of Community Psychology*, *67*(3–4), 312–326.

Rose, D. (2018). Participatory research: Real or imagined. *Social Psychiatry and Psychiatric Epidemiology*, *53*(8), 765–771.

Rose, D. (2020). On personal epiphanies and collective knowledge in survivor research and action. *Social Theory & Health*, *18*(2), 110–122.

Rose, D. S. (2022). Mental challenges as constitutive of marginalisation? In D. S. Rose (Ed.), *Mad knowledges and user-led research* (pp. 31–62). Palgrave Macmillan.

Rose, D., Evans, J., Sweeney, A., & Wykes, T. (2011). A model for developing outcome measures from the perspectives of mental health service users. *International Review of Psychiatry*, *23*(1), 41–46.

Rose, D., & Kalathil, J. (2019). Power, privilege and knowledge: The untenable promise of co-production in mental "health". *Frontiers in Sociology*, *4*, 57.

Rose, T. (2016). *The end of average: How to succeed in a world that values sameness*. Penguin.

Rosqvist, H. B., Botha, M., Hens, K., O'Donoghue, S., Pearson, A., & Stenning, A. (2023). Cutting our own keys: New possibilities of neurodivergent storying in research. *Autism*, *27*(5), 1235–1244.

Rosqvist, H. B., Kourti, M., Jackson-Perry, D., Brownlow, C., Fletcher, K., Bendelman, D., & O'Dell, L. (2019). Doing it differently: Emancipatory autism studies within a neurodiverse academic space. *Disability & Society*, *34*(7–8), 1082–1101.

Rosqvist, H. B., Örulv, L., Hasselblad, S., Hansson, D., Nilsson, K., & Seng, H. (2020). Designing an autistic space for research: Exploring the impact of context, space, and sociality in autistic writing processes. In H. Rosqvist, N. Chown, & A. Stenning (Eds.), *Neurodiversity Studies: A new critical paradigm* (pp. 156–171). Routledge.

Rost, M., Favaretto, M., & De Clercq, E. (2022). Normality in medicine: An empirical elucidation. *Philosophy, Ethics, and Humanities in Medicine*, *17*(1), 1–14.

Rouse, A., Armstrong, J., & McLeod, J. (2015). Enabling connections: Counsellor creativity and therapeutic practice. *Counselling and Psychotherapy Research*, *15*(3), 171–179.

Roy, N. (2022). The use of indigenous research methodologies in counselling: Responsibility, respect, relationality, and reciprocity. *First Peoples Child & Family Review*, *17*(1), 3–19.

Russell, C. (2020). *Rekindling democracy: A Professional's guide to working in citizen space*. Cascade Books.

Russo, J., & Beresford, P. (2015). Between exclusion and colonisation: Seeking a place for mad people's knowledge in academia. *Disability & Society*, *30*(1), 153–157.

Russo, J., & Sweeney, A. (Eds.) (2016). *Searching for a rose garden. Challenging psychiatry, fostering mad studies*. PCCS Books.

Sanchez-Youngman, S., & Wallerstein, N. (2018). Partnership river of life: Creating a historical timeline. In N. Wallerstein, B. Duran, J. Oetzel, & M. Minkler (Eds.), *Community-based participatory research for health: Advancing health equity*. 2nd ed. Jossey Bass.

Saunkeah, B., Beans, J. A., Peercy, M. T., Hiratsuka, V. Y., & Spicer, P. (2021). Extending research protections to tribal communities. *The American Journal of Bioethics, 21*(10), 5–12.

Schoonenboom, J. (2024). A performative approach to mixed methods research. In Y. Shan (Ed.), *Philosophical Foundations of Mixed Methods Research* (pp. 127–151). Routledge.

Scottish Dementia Working Group Research Sub-Group, UK. (2014). Core principles for involving people with dementia in research. *Dementia, 13*(5), 680–685.

Seikkula, J., & Trimble, D. (2005). Healing elements of therapeutic conversation: Dialogue as an embodiment of love. *Family Process, 44*(4), 461–475.

Sen, A. (2010). *The idea of justice*. Penguin.

Sharmil, H., Kelly, J., Bowden, M., Galletly, C., Cairney, I., Wilson, C., ... & de Crespigny, C. (2021). Participatory action research-Dadirri-Ganma, using yarning: Methodology co-design with Aboriginal community members. *International Journal for Equity in Health, 20*(1), 1–11.

Sharp, A. M. (1987). What is a 'Community of Inquiry'? *Journal of Moral Education, 16*(1), 37–45.

Shdaimah, C. S., & McGarry, B. (2018). Social workers' use of moral entrepreneurship to enact professional ethics in the field: Case studies from the social justice profession. *British Journal of Social Work, 48*(1), 21–36.

Shillingford, M., Oh, S., & DiLorenzo, A. (2018). Using the multiphase model of psychotherapy, school counseling, human rights, and social justice to support haitian immigrant students. *Professional Counselor, 8*(3), 240–248.

Shimmin, C., Wittmeier, K. D., Lavoie, J. G., Wicklund, E. D., & Sibley, K. M. (2017). Moving towards a more inclusive patient and public involvement in health research paradigm: The incorporation of a trauma-informed intersectional analysis. *BMC Health Services Research, 17*(1), 1–10.

Sieber, J. E., & Tolich, M. B. (2013) *Planning ethically responsible research*. 2nd edn. Sage.

Silverio, S. A., Wilkinson, C., & Wilkinson, S. (2022). Academic ventriloquism: Tensions between inclusion, representation, and anonymity in qualitative research. In P. Liamputtong (Ed.), *Handbook of social inclusion: Research and practices in health and social sciences* (pp. 642–660). Springer.

Sitter, K. C. (2017). Taking a closer look at photovoice as a participatory action research method. *Journal of Progressive Human Services, 28*(1), 36–48.

Skop, M. (2016). The art of body mapping: A methodological guide for social work researchers. *Aotearoa New Zealand Social Work, 28*(4), 29–43.

Slote, K. Y., Cuthbert, C., Mesh, C. J., Driggers, M. G., Bancroft, L., & Silverman, J. G. (2005). Battered mothers speak out: Participatory human rights documentation as a model for research and activism in the United States. *Violence Against Women, 11*(11), 1367–1395.

Smith, A. J., Hallum-Montes, R., Nevin, K., Zenker, R., Sutherland, B., Reagor, S., ... & Brennan, J. M. (2018). Determinants of transgender individuals' well-being, mental health, and suicidality in a rural state. *Journal of Rural Mental Health, 42*(2), 116.

Smith, K., McLeod, J., Blunden, N., Cooper, M., Gabriel, L., Kupfer, C., ... & Winter, L. A. (2021). A pluralistic perspective on research in psychotherapy: Harnessing passion, difference and dialogue to promote justice and relevance. *Frontiers in Psychology*, 3728. https://doi.org/10.3389/fpsyg.2021.742676

Smith, L. T. (2021). *Decolonizing methodologies: Research and indigenous peoples*. Bloomsbury Publishing.

Smith, P., Simpson, L., & Madill, A. (2021). Service user experiences of a novel in-reach rehabilitation and recovery service for people with profound and enduring mental health needs. *International Journal of Mental Health Nursing, 30*(5), 1106–1116.

Soggiu, A. S., Eirik Karlsson, B., Gøril Klevan, T., & Ness, O. (2021). Inner and outer voices in research: How dialogical approaches can enhance knowledge development in mental healthcare. *Australian and New Zealand Journal of Family Therapy, 42*(2), 225–240.

Sood, S., Cronin, C., & Kostizak, K. (2018). *Participatory research toolkit.* Rain Barrel Communications. https://static1.squarespace.com/static/5df678c23b758e75366c17cd/t/5e65c84187bd3863b8389431/1583728710133/Participatory+Research+Toolkit+Rain+Barrel+Communications.pdf (accessed 16th February 2023).

Southby, K. (2017). Reflecting on (the challenge of) conducting participatory research as a research-degree student. *Research for All, 1*(1), 128–142.

Speciale, M., Gess, J., & Speedlin, S. (2015). You don't look like a lesbian: A coautoethnography of intersectional identities in counselor education. *Journal of LGBT Issues in Counseling, 9*(4), 256–272.

Spong, S., & Waters, R. (2015). Community-based participatory research in counselling and psychotherapy. *European Journal of Psychotherapy & Counselling, 17*(1), 5–20.

Springham, N., & Xenophontes, I. (2021). Democratising the discourse: Co-production in art therapy practice, research and publication. *International Journal of Art Therapy, 26*(1–2), 1–7.

Srinath, S., & Bhola, P. (2016) Research ethics in psychotherapy and psychosocial interventions: Role of institutional ethical review boards. In P. Bhola & A. Raguram (Eds.), *Ethical issues in counselling and psychotherapy practice* (pp. 219–238). Springer.

Staniszewska, S., Brett, J., Simera, I., Seers, K., Mockford, C., Goodlad, S., ... & Tysall, C. (2017). GRIPP2 reporting checklists: Tools to improve reporting of patient and public involvement in research. *British Medical Journal, 358.* https://doi.org/10.1136/bmj.j3453

Stark, E., Ali, D., Ayre, A., Schneider, N., Parveen, S., Marais, K., ... & Pender, R. (2021). Coproduction with autistic adults: Reflections from the authentistic research collective. *Autism in Adulthood, 3*(2), 195–203.

Stewart, J., & Zediker, K. (2000). Dialogue as tensional, ethical practice. *Southern Communication Journal, 65*, 224–242.

Stige, S. H., Barca, T., Lavik, K. O., & Moltu, C. (2021). Barriers and facilitators in adolescent psychotherapy initiated by adults—experiences that differentiate adolescents' trajectories through mental health care. *Frontiers in Psychology, 12.* doi: 10.3389/fpsyg.2021.633663

Stirling, F. J., & Chandler, A. (2021). Dangerous arms and everyday activism: A dialogue between two researchers with lived experience of self-harm. *International Review of Qualitative Research, 14*(1), 155–170.

Stone, E., & Priestley, M. (1996). Parasites, pawns and partners: Disability research and the role of non-disabled researchers. *British Journal of Sociology, 47*, 699–716.

Sunderland, N., Catalana, T., Kendall, E., McAuliffe, D., & Chenoweth, L. (2010). Exploring the concept of moral distress with community based researchers: An Australian study. *Journal of Social Service Research, 37*, 73–85.

Swarbrick, C. M., Doors, O., Scottish Dementia Working Group, EDUCATE, Davis, K., & Keady, J. (2019). Visioning change: Co-producing a model of involvement and engagement in research. *Dementia, 18*(7–8), 3165–3172.

Sweeney, A. (2021). *Evidence-based guidelines for conducting trauma-informed talking therapy assessments.* Kings College, London. https://www.kcl.ac.uk/ioppn/assets/trauma-informed-assessment-guidelines.pdf (accessed 13th February 2023).

Sweeney, A., Clement, S., Gribble, K., Jackson, E., Carr, S., Catty, J., & Gillard, S. (2019). A systematic review of qualitative studies of adults' experiences of being assessed for psychological therapies. *Health Expectations*, *22*(2), 133–148.

Sweeney, A., Greenwood, K. E., Williams, S., Wykes, T., & Rose, D. S. (2013). Hearing the voices of service user researchers in collaborative qualitative data analysis: The case for multiple coding. *Health Expectations*, *16*(4), e89–e99.

Sweeney, A., Kelly, K., Kennedy, A., Clement, S., Ion, M., Kothari, G., & Gillard, S. (2022). Balancing closeness and distance through identity enactment: Psychological therapy assessments explored through the assessor-client dyad. *Qualitative Research in Psychology*, *19*(3), 722–746.

Sweeney, A., & Taggart, D. (2018). (Mis) understanding trauma-informed approaches in mental health. *Journal of Mental Health*, *27*(5), 383–387.

Sweeney, A., White, S., Kelly, K., Faulkner, A., Papoulias, S., & Gillard, S. (2022). Survivor-led guidelines for conducting trauma-informed psychological therapy assessments: Development and modified Delphi study. *Health Expectations*, *25*(6), 2818–2827.

Sysling, F. (2021). Phrenology and the average person, 1840–1940. *History of the Human Sciences*, *34*(2), 27–45.

Tasca, G. A., Ravitz, P., Hunter, J., Chyurlia, L., Baker, S., Balfour, L., Mcquaid, N., Pain, C., Compare, A., Brugnera, A., & Leszcz, M. (2023). Training community-based psychotherapists to maintain a therapeutic alliance: A psychotherapy practice research network study. *Psychotherapy*, *60*(1), 98–109.

Tauri, J. M. (2018). Research ethics, informed consent and the disempowerment of First Nation peoples. *Research Ethics*, *14*(3), 1–14.

Thomas, F., Hansford, L., Wyatt, K., Byng, R., Coombes, K., Finch, J., & Stuteley, H. (2020). An engaged approach to exploring issues around poverty and mental health: A reflective evaluation of the research process from researchers and community partners involved in the DeStress study. *Health Expectations*, *24*(S1), 113–121.

Thomas, F., Wyatt, K., & Hansford, L. (2020). The violence of narrative: Embodying responsibility for poverty-related stress. *Sociology of Health & Illness*, *42*(5), 1123–1138.

Thomas, K. A., Goodman, L. A., Vainer, E. S., Heimel, D., Barkai, R., & Collins-Gousby, D. (2018). "No sacred cows or bulls": The story of the domestic violence program evaluation and research collaborative (DVPERC). *Journal of Family Violence*, *33*(8), 537–549.

Tillmann-Healy, L. M. (2003). Friendship as method. *Qualitative Inquiry*, *9*(5), 729–749.

Tootell, A. (2004). Decentring research practice. *International Journal of Narrative Therapy & Community Work*, *2004*(3), 54–60.

Topa, W., & Narvaez, D. (2022). *Restoring the kinship worldview: Indigenous voices introduce 28 precepts for rebalancing life on planet earth*. North Atlantic Books.

Trachsel, M., & grosse Holtforth, M. (2019). How to strengthen patients' meaning response by an ethical informed consent in psychotherapy. *Frontiers in Psychology*, *10*, 1747.

Tronto, J. C. (1993). *Moral boundaries: A political argument for an ethic of care*. Psychology Press.

Tronto, J. C. (2013). *Caring democracy: Markets, equality, and justice*. New York University Press.

Tuck, E., & Yang, K. W. (2012). Decolonization is not a metaphor. *Education & Society*, *1*(1), 1–40.

Tuia, T. T., & Cobb, D. (2021). Decolonizing Samoan fa'afaletui methodology: Taking a closer look. *AlterNative: An International Journal of Indigenous Peoples*, *17*(2), 275–283.

Turner, K., & Gillard, S. (2012). Still out there? Is the service user voice becoming lost as user involvement moves into the mental health research mainstream? In M. Barnes & P. Cotterell (Eds.), *Critical perspectives on user involvement* (pp.189–201). Policy Press.

Valdez-Martínez, E., & Bedolla, M. (2020). Research and research ethics committees and the obligation for them to operate in accordance with the principle of the social covenant. *Gaceta Médica de México, 156*, 138–141.

Van Katwyk, T., & Guzik, C. (2022). Qualitative research: Using collaborative critical autoethnography to decolonise through "seeing" and doing: Social work, community engagement, and ethical practice. *Aotearoa New Zealand Social Work, 34*(2), 67–80.

Van Katwyk, T., & Seko, Y. (2017). Knowing through improvisational dance: A collaborative autoethnography. *Forum Qualitative Sozialforschung/Forum: Qualitative Social Research, 18*, 2.

Vat, L. E., Ryan, D., & Etchegary, H. (2017). Recruiting patients as partners in health research: A qualitative descriptive study. *Research Involvement and Engagement, 3*, 1–14.

Veseth, M., Binder, P. E., Borg, M., & Davidson, L. (2016). Recovery in bipolar disorders: Experienced therapists' view of their patients' struggles and efforts when facing a severe mental illness. *Journal of Psychotherapy Integration, 26*(4), 437.

Veseth, M., Binder, P. E., Borg, M., & Davidson, L. (2017). Collaborating to stay open and aware: Service user involvement in mental health research as an aid in reflexivity. *Nordic Psychology, 69*(4), 256–263.

Viney, W. (2022). *William James's pluralism: An antidote for contemporary extremism and* absolutism. Routledge.

Vojtila, L., Ashfaq, I., Ampofo, A., Dawson, D., & Selby, P. (2021). Engaging a person with lived experience of mental illness in a collaborative care model feasibility study. *Research Involvement and Engagement, 7*(1), 1–8.

von Peter, S., & Bos, G. F. (2022). The necessity of unsettling encounters in collaborative research. Reflections of two researchers without experiential expertise. *Collaborations: A Journal of Community-Based Research and Practice, 5*(1). https://doi.org/10.33596/ coll.78

Waddell-Henowitch, C., Gobeil, J., Tacan, F., Ford, M., Herron, R. V., Allan, J. A., ... & Spence, S. (2022). A collaborative multi-method approach to evaluating Indigenous land-based learning with men. *International Journal of Qualitative Methods, 21*, 16094069221082359.

Waddell, C. M., de Jager, M. D., Gobeil, J., Tacan, F., Herron, R. V., Allan, J. A., & Roger, K. (2021). Healing journeys: Indigenous Men's reflections on resources and barriers to mental wellness. *Social Science & Medicine, 270*, 113696.

Wallerstein, M. M., Sanchez-Youngman, S., Rodriguez-Espinosa, P., Avila, M., Baker, E. E., Barnett, S., Belone, L., Golub, M., Lucero, J., Mahdi, I., Noyes, E., Nguyen, T., Roubideaux, Y., Sigo, R., & Duran, B. (2019). Power dynamics in community- based participatory research: A multiple-case study analysis of partnering contexts, histories, and practices. *Health Education & Behavior, 46*(IS), 19S–32S.

Walter, M. M. (2010). The politics of the data: How the Australian statistical Indigene is constructed. *International Journal of Critical Indigenous Studies, 3*(2), 45–56.

Walter, M., & Suina, M. (2019). Indigenous data, indigenous methodologies and indigenous data sovereignty. *International Journal of Social Research Methodology, 22*(3), 233–243.

Wampold, B. E., & Flückiger, C. (2023). The alliance in mental health care: Conceptualization, evidence and clinical applications. *World Psychiatry, 22*(1), 25–41.

Wang, C., & Burris, M. A. (1994). Empowerment through photo novella: Portraits of participation. *Health Education Quarterly, 21*(2), 171–186.

Warwick-Booth, L., Bagnall, A. M., & Coan, S. (2021). *Creating participatory research: Principles, practice and reality*. Policy Press.

Waters, R., Spong, S., Morgan, J., & Kemp-Philp, C. (2018). Carers' beliefs about counselling: A community participatory study in Wales. *British Journal of Guidance & Counselling, 46*(2), 160–172.

Weinberg, M., & Banks, S. (2019). Practising ethically in unethical times: Everyday resistance in social work. *Ethics and Social Welfare,13*(4), 361–376.

Wendt, D. C., Huson, K., Albatnuni, M., & Gone, J. P. (2022). What are the best practices for psychotherapy with indigenous peoples in the United States and Canada? A thorny question. *Journal of Consulting and Clinical Psychology, 90*(10), 802–814.

West, W. (1996). Using human inquiry groups in counselling research. *British Journal of Guidance and Counselling, 24*, 347–355.

West, W. (1997). Integrating counselling, psychotherapy and healing: An inquiry into counsellors and psychotherapists whose works includes healing. *British Journal of Guidance and Counselling, 25*(3), 291–312.

Wilkinson, C. (2018). Are you telling me this as a researcher or a friend? Ethical issues for a UK doctoral researcher. In S. Banks & M. Brydon-Miller (Eds.), *Ethics in participatory research for health and social well-being* (pp. 66–69). Routledge.

Wilkinson, H. (2001). Including people with dementia in research. In H. Wilkinson (Ed.), *The perspectives of people with dementia: Research methods and motivations* (pp. 9–25). Jessica Kingsley.

Williams, G. L. (2020). From anonymous subject to engaged stakeholder: Enriching participant experience in autistic-language-use research. *Research for All, 4*(2), 314–328.

Wilson, E., Kenny, A., & Dickson-Swift, V. (2018). Ethical challenges of community based participatory research: exploring researchers' experience. *International Journal of Social Research Methodology, 21*(1), 7–24.

Wilson, S. (2008). *Research is ceremony: Indigenous research methods*. Fernwood Publishing.

Winter, L., & Charura, D. (Eds.) (2023). *The SAGE handbook of social justice in the psychological therapies*. Sage.

Woodgate, R. L., Zurba, M. & Tennent, P. (2017). Worth a thousand words? Advantages, challenges and opportunities in working with photovoice as a qualitative research method with youth and their families. *Forum Qualitative Sozialforschung/Forum: Qualitative Social Research, 18*, 1.

Worsley, J. D., McKeown, M., Wilson, T., & Corcoran, R. (2022). A qualitative evaluation of coproduction of research: "If you do it properly, you will get turbulence". *Health Expectations, 25*(5), 2034–2042.

Wyness, L. (2015). "Talking of citizenship…" Exploring the contribution an intergenerational, participatory learning project can make to the promotion of active citizenship in sustainable communities. *Local Environment, 20*(3), 277–297.

Yalom, I. D., & Elkin, G. (2008). *Every day gets a little closer: A twice-told therapy*. Basic Books.

Yang, N., Jankauskaite, G., Gerstenblith, J. A., Hillman, J. W., Wang, R. J., Le, T. P., & Hill, C. E. (2023). Counseling psychology doctoral students' experiences of authenticity: A collaborative autoethnography. *Counselling Psychology Quarterly, 36*(1), 89–111.

Youn, S. J., Xiao, H., McAleavey, A. A., Scofield, B. E., Pedersen, T. R., Castonguay, L. G., ... & Locke, B. D. (2019). Assessing and investigating clinicians' research interests: Lessons on expanding practices and data collection in a large practice research network. *Psychotherapy, 56*(1), 67–82.

Yunkaporta, T. (2019). *Sand talk: How Indigenous thinking can save the world.* Text Publishing.

Yunkaporta, T., & Moodie, D. (2021). Thought ritual: An Indigenous data analysis method for research. In T. McKenna, D. Moodie, & P. Onesta (Eds.), *Indigenous knowledges: privileging our voices* (pp. 87–96). Brill.

Index

For Product Safety Concerns and Information please contact our EU
representative GPSR@taylorandfrancis.com
Taylor & Francis Verlag GmbH, Kaufingerstraße 24, 80331 München, Germany

www.ingramcontent.com/pod-product-compliance
Lightning Source LLC
Chambersburg PA
CBHW052011270326
41929CB00015B/2879

* 9 7 8 1 0 3 2 5 2 2 6 1 6 *